HOME DECORATING

Mike Lawrence

The Crowood Press

First published in 1991 by
The Crowood Press Ltd
Ramsbury, Marlborough
Wiltshire SN8 2HR

New edition 2002

British Library Cataloguing-in-Publication Data
A catalogue record for this book is available from the British Library.

ISBN 1 86126 551 4

Acknowledgements

Line drawings by Andrew Green.

The author would like to thank the following companies and organizations for providing the photographs listed below:

Black & Decker (pages 18, 71, 73 and 75); Blue Hawk (pages 8 and 45); Crown Paints (pages 65 and 67); Douglas Kane (page 29); Dulux (pages 9 and 85); Evode (page 11); H & R Johnson (page 8); Marley Floors (pages 9, 35 and 59); Marshall Cavendish (pages 12, 14–18, 87 and 91); Richard Burbidge (page 41); Sikkens (page 7); Swish (page 57); Vitrex Tools (page 18); Wickes Building Supplies (pages 10, 13, 55 and 62).

Typeset by Acuté, Stroud, Gloucestershire
Printed and bound by Times Offset (M) Sdn. Bhd.

Contents

Introduction

Decorating your home is one of the most popular of all do-it-yourself activities, with around 90 per cent of all house holders tackling at least some decorating jobs at some time. But it was not always so. Until the 1920s and 1930s painting, paper-hanging and other decorative trades were very much the province of the professional, and it is only in the last thirty or forty years that doing your own home decorating has become so commonplace.

Several factors are responsible for the rise of the amateur decorator. The rapid growth in home ownership since the 1950s is one, coupled with a steady increase in leisure time and a growing disinclination to pay the increasingly expensive prices charged by professionals in every sphere of home improvement. All this has been greatly aided and abetted by the intro-duction of a whole host of new decorating materials formulated to allow the amateur to get good results without the need for a high level of skill. The result is that many people can now boast of a home which they have decorated from top to bottom themselves, and the less keen or able can wield a paintbrush with confidence even if they still prefer to leave the intricacies of hanging and matching wallpaper, tiling the bathroom wall or laying new carpets to an expert.

This book is written with the keen and able beginner, rather than the experienced home decorator in mind. Its aim is to explain the basic techniques first, and then to show how these can be applied to a whole host of decorating jobs inside and outside the house. It also tells you about all the various materials you can use, and how to prepare surfaces so you get good results when working with them.

Many decorating jobs are not technically difficult, and decorating materials are by and large relatively inexpensive. What often puts many people off tackling the work themselves is the scale of the job and the time it is likely to take – yet it is this high time and labour content that makes home decorating so worthwhile in financial terms.

As an example, the cost of employing a professional for a typical job such as redecorating a room by stripping and re-placing the wallpaper and repainting the ceiling and the woodwork is roughly five times the bill for materials. All you need to save the money is your own unpaid spare time – say 40 hours for a 4m (13ft) square room – and, more importantly, the wish to do the work and to enjoy doing it. This book will help to give you the know-how; the pleasure at completing a par-ticular job will be all yours.

THE BASICS

There is a lot to decorate in the average house, and the best way to gauge what is involved in your home is take a guided tour around the property.

Start at the front door, and cast yourself in the role of a prospective purchaser trying to take an objective view of the overall decorative effect. The colour schemes used in different rooms will strike you first of all, both individually as colours you like or dislike, and then collectively as pleasing or jarring combinations. You may also notice the use of many different materials and the effect they have on making rooms seem light and airy, warm and cosy or dull and dingy.

As you progress round the house, you will begin to form another impression . . . of the overall condition of your decorations. Nothing looks worse than a house that seems uncared-for, with chipped or flaking paintwork, dowdy old-fashioned wallcoverings, ceilings that are discoloured and criss-crossed with cracks, floor coverings with worn patches and lifting seams. You can easily get used to living in rooms that are beginning to show their age, and by looking at them through the eyes of a stranger you will get a new perspective on the state of things.

What to Tackle Indoors

Don't let your guided tour depress you unduly; the object of the exercise is to evaluate what you want to achieve in your home. You may find that some rooms are already decorated to your satisfaction, while others could, if you were honest, definitely do with a face-lift.

Decorating differs from most other DIY jobs in that it is often done on a whim rather than out of necessity. People *like* redecorating their home every so often in much the same way as they crave a new set of clothes: for a change of look. The old gear may not be worn out, but fashions and tastes change. So may the family's needs - a bedroom for a five-year-old will be decorated very differently when he or she becomes a teenager, and a living room or bathroom will change its role dramatically when the children leave home.

The best way of working out what you

want, or need, to do is to walk round the house room by room, looking at the way each is decorated now and asking yourself if it looks the way you want it to. Here are some questions to ask yourself and some observations to make as you go along.

The entrance hall Your front door and entrance hall set the tone for the whole property. What will visitors think of yours? Is it bright and welcoming or dark and gloomy? You will not be able to do much about its shape, but you can use decorative tricks like foreshortening a long narrow corridor by painting the end wall in a darker shade to the rest of the hall. Does the stairwell dominate the hall? Changing the way it is decorated and carpeted could help it blend in better. And is the hall floorcovering practical? It will have to withstand the passage of feet in all sorts of weather, so will need to be hardwearing and easy to clean.

Fig 1 (*above*) Acquiring some basic decorating skills will allow you to tackle a wide range of home decorating jobs.

What to Tackle

The living room This can be the most difficult room to decorate successfully because it is used for two potentially conflicting purposes – private relaxation and public entertainment. The Victorians solved this problem brilliantly by living in the back parlour and keeping the front room 'for best', but nowadays few homes can spare an extra room purely for show. So today's living rooms must blend warmth and comfort with durability and practicality, offering a fresh lively atmosphere by day and a cosy and peaceful one by night.

Often the key to success lies in the use of flexible lighting, but the decorations play a vital part too. How do they blend in with the furniture, the floorcovering, the carpets? Do they need to coordinate with the colour scheme in adjoining rooms such as through dining areas? Are there any interesting features such as alcoves, an archway, even an attractive cornice that you want to highlight, or ugly features such as high ceilings that you want to disguise? Is the way the furniture is arranged sensible, or does it impede access into or through the room?

The dining room As one of the least used of your 'habitable' rooms (as opposed to service rooms such as the kitchen or bathroom), this often gets sadly neglected. It needs to provide a pleasant setting for just one activity, eating, so it should combine a restful colour scheme (to avoid visual 'indigestion') with some adjustable lighting so that tables can be laid in good light and meals eaten in a dimmer light.

The kitchen Hygiene is the watchword in the kitchen: because of the amount of moisture and airborne grease generated by cooking, washing up and the like, every surface must be easy to clean. Are yours? Looks are also important, especially to the family cook slaving over a hot stove, so it makes sense to decorate the room in a way that lends itself to regular redecoration as a means of changing the scenery.

Nowadays there is a trend away from the clinical 'operating theatre' kitchen with its smooth laminates and steel fittings, and back to what we imagine the Victorian country kitchen resembled – lots of natural timber, curtains at the windows instead of blinds and rush matting on the quarry tiles. If you plan to allow yourself to be

seduced by this image, keep the practicalities of running a kitchen to the fore.

Bedrooms These are the most personal of rooms in the house, and should be decorated to reflect the taste of their occupants. After all, we each spend more time each day in our bedrooms than in any other room of the house. Also, uniquely, we see the room from two different viewpoints – on entering, and when lying in bed – so colour schemes and decorative features need to bear this in mind. Floor coverings should be kind to bare feet, yet in children's rooms must be tough enough to withstand rough and tumble and the occasional liquid disaster. Such rooms should also be geared to ease of redecoration at regular intervals as a child's taste changes with age.

Fig 2 (*above*) Inside the house there are plenty of different surfaces that need decorating – the ceilings, the walls, the floors and the woodwork – and plenty of options for each one.

Fig 3 (*left*) Some rooms such as bathrooms need decorations that are tough enough to withstand wear and damp conditions while being welcoming to the eye.

What to Tackle

The bathroom This room has special needs, particularly if you have children. It must look and feel warm, yet must be decorated with wall- and floorcoverings able to cope with steam and splashes, and capable of being cleaned easily. Does yours meet these criteria? If not, a more sensible choice of materials could go a long way to solving your problems.

The interior as a whole As you make your guided tour, take note of obvious problem areas – those that have to endure heavy wear, for example. If you find floorcoverings wearing badly or scuff marks and knocks to the paintwork round doorways or on staircases, choosing different materials when you redecorate could help avoid the problem in the future. Look out too for areas that seem to harbour dirt or suffer from condensation or staining, so you can eliminate any underlying problems before you start redecorating.

You will now be considerably wiser about the decorative condition of your house, and also more motivated about how to go about redecorating it. You will have seen it as a whole rather than a series of disjointed parts, and this makes it much easier to evolve a plan for a home that is attractively decorated and has a sense of style about it. You will also be much more aware of the range of materials at present in use around the house, and about how well they suit your particular lifestyle.

have been decorated – and how successfully. This gives you an opportunity to see how well different ideas and colour schemes work in practice without having to go to the trouble and expense of trying it out on your own home and perhaps making an expensive mistake.

Fig 4 (*above*) What you put on your floors depends on whether you want comfort, durability or both.

Fig 5 (*below*) Out of doors, your main task lies in decorating the woodwork, but outside walls may be painted too.

What to Tackle Outdoors

You obviously have less scope for being creative with the exterior decoration of your home, especially if it has brick or stone walls. Woodwork will either be painted or stained, and even rendered or timber-clad walls will generally be painted in one colour. Your first priority will be to ensure that everything is in good condition, so your house looks smart and well looked-after. Then you can start thinking about whether to give it an air of individuality by some judicious use of colour; there is no law that says everyone must have white walls or brown stained woodwork, although you would think that there was from the appearance of many a modern estate!

The best way of discovering what works and what doesn't is to look around your area and see how other houses like yours

The material you are likely to use most of when decorating your house is paint. We have been painting the walls of our homes for centuries, but never before have the paints been so good at their job. The latest product of paint-making technology is a paint that promises one-coat cover over *almost* anything – about as far as we can go towards effortless decorating. All the paints currently on the market offer good covering power, excellent durability and a huge range of colours.

Paint for Walls and Ceilings

The biggest seller is what everyone calls emulsion paint – literally a suspension of pigment and binder droplets in water. When you apply it, the water evaporates leaving behind a film which itself reacts chemically as it hardens to form a tough, protective surface layer. The finish may be non-reflective (matt) or slightly shiny (satin or silk finish). Most emulsions sold for DIY use are non-drip, making it easier to apply them in thicker coats without the paint running down the wall and dripping off the brush.

Some people – notably the decorating trade – still swear by 'ordinary' runny emulsion, probably for two reaons: they have the skill to apply it without runs or drips occurring, and it is slightly cheaper than non-drip types. The choice of which to use is entirely up to you.

There is a third choice, known as 'solid' emulsion and developed mainly for use on ceilings, although there is no reason why you shouldn't use it on walls too. It comes in a rectangular tray, and you put it on with a roller – it is too thick to brush out properly. The idea is to minimize the drips and splashes that usually result from using a paint roller with ordinary emulsion, although you will still be wise to use dust sheets when applyingit.

Special exterior-quality emulsion paints are also used on exterior walls; they contain a fungicide to guard against mould growth, and often have added fillers to help them bridge small cracks.

Apart from ease of application, the other advantages of emulsion paints are that they do not smell too strongly when you are using them, they dry quickly, and they can be cleaned from equipment simply with water. They can also be overpainted quickly and cheaply when you want a change of colour scheme.

Fig 6 (*above*) Paint in all its varieties and colours is the mainstay of most interior and exterior decorating jobs.

Of course, you do not *have* to use emulsion paint on walls and ceilings; there is no reason why you should not use the sort of paints normally reserved for decorating woodwork and metalwork (*see below*), and until the development of durable wall paints it was common for walls at least to be painted in this way. Certainly such paints will be rather more durable than emulsions, but set against this is the fact that they are generally more difficult for the amateur decorator to apply evenly to large areas, and they are less tolerant of poorly-prepared surfaces. They also cost more.

Paint for Wood and Metal

When it comes to decorating woodwork and metalwork around the house, most do-it-yourselfers tend to go for a traditional finish – gloss paint. The main difference between this and emulsion paint is that the pigment and binder are dissolved in a petroleum-based solvent instead of being suspended in water. This means that the paint takes longer to dry than emulsion and as the solvent evaporates there is a strong 'painty' smell which many people find unpleasant and to which some are actually allergic. However, the resulting film is tougher than emulsion, making this type of paint the ideal choice for surfaces which get a lot of heavy wear or regular handling – doors, windows, staircases and furniture, for example.

The other drawback with solvent-based

paints is that they are intrinsically more difficult to apply successfully than emulsions, for two reasons. The first is that they are not a one-coat product (except when you are redecorating an already-painted surface); you have to prepare the bare surface by applying a primer and, in some cases, an undercoat as well, before putting on the final decorative finish. This is time-consuming, although paint manufacturers have tried to get round the problem by formulating one-coat primer/ undercoats and, most recently, self-undercoating gloss. The second problem is that actually getting a smooth, even finish to the surface you are painting is trickier with solvent-based paints; good technique is all-important.

'Gloss' paints actually come with either a high gloss or a more subtle semi-matt or eggshell finish, often called satin or silk by the manufacturers. These semi-matt paints have the advantage that they tend to disguise blemishes on less than perfect surfaces. Choose whichever finish you prefer.

As with emulsion paints, you also have a choice between non-drip or 'runny' types. The non-drip versions allow you to apply a thicker coat without the risk of the paint running or sagging, often enabling you to get away with a one-coat finish, and are more forgiving of less than perfect brushwork. However, they tend to be a little more expensive than the runny types.

There is one last snag – cleaning up afterwards. With ordinary solvent-based paints, you have to use a solvent such as white spirit or a proprietary brush cleaner to remove paint from your decorating equipment, and this can be a messy and difficult business if the paint has begun to harden. Some paints have a special additive which is supposed to allow you to wash the paint out with hot soapy water, but this works only if the paint is still wet; after a long painting session you will find you still have to use solvent to get rid of all the paint.

You can use these paints on metal too, so long as you use the right primer (see page 87 for more details). An alternative is to go for self-priming paints, which can also cope with any surface rusting. These paints are also available in aerosol form — useful for decorating awkward surfaces such as gates and metal railings that are difficult to paint with a brush.

Clear Finishes for Wood

Many people prefer to give wood fittings and furniture a finish that enhances the grain pattern and colour of the wood, instead of obscuring it as paint does. Varnishes are the product to use.

Varnish is basically a solvent-based paint without the pigment (although there are some solvent-free water-based varnishes now beginning to find their way onto the market). The commonest type is based on polyurethane resins; these are very hardwearing and so are ideal for surfaces such as floors and furniture. However, if they are used out of doors they are not easy to re-coat satisfactorily once they have been weathered, and many decorators prefer to use traditional oil or alkyd resin varnishes instead.

Where the wood colour is weak or you want to colour the surface without obscuring the grain, you can either stain the wood before applying varnish to it, or else use a pigmented varnish known as a coloured sealer. The latter is quicker to use, but does not give the same depth of colour as wood stain and varnish used separately.

Stains for use on wood are either spirit-based or water-based, and both types come in a wide range of wood shades and primary colours. You can inter-mix different shades of the same stain type to achieve the exact colour you want, and both can be diluted with the appropriate solvent (white spirit for spirit-based stains, water for water-based ones) to weaken the colour depth.

Fig 7 (*left*) There is now a huge range of varnishes and stains available for every timber surface.

Wallcoverings

After paint, wallcoverings of various types will be your second-largest home decorating purchase. Although you probably choose a new wallcovering mainly because you like the colour or design, it's important to remember that you need performance as well as decoration, especially in rooms where the walls are likely to suffer more than their fair share of wear and tear. Here is a guide to help you choose the right type for the job.

Wallcoverings to Paint

The idea of hanging a wallcovering and then painting over it may sound like making two jobs out of one. It certainly adds to the time the job takes the first time you do it, but you recoup that in the future when redecorating means simply applying another coat of paint.

Lining paper is not really meant to be used as a wallcovering in its own right; its main purpose is in providing a smooth surface for hanging other wallcoverings. However, it is a cheap way of covering up plaster that is full of hairline cracks although it won't hide major lumps and bumps. Look for the extra-white grade, which is designed for overpainting; other grades have a somewhat hairy surface that does not take paint so well.

Woodchip paper is a coarse pulpy paper with small chips of wood embedded in it, and once painted has the texture of coarse oatmeal. It's very good at hiding defects in walls and ceilings, and once it has been overpainted a few times it is quite hard-wearing too. There are several weights available, with the heavier types having the coarser chips.

Relief wallcoverings have a surface carrying random or regular embossed designs, and may be made from paper (Anaglypta and similar products), cotton fibres (Anaglypta SupaDurable) or vinyl on a paper backing (Anaglypta Luxury Vinyl and similar brands. Types with a repeat pattern mean you can have 'design' with your colour, and all are excellent at disguising poor surfaces. Care needs to be taken when hanging the cheaper, light types, because over-soaking and careless handling can flatten the embossing irreversibly. However, cotton and vinyl types are virtually indestructible, and the vinyl

types have the added advantage of being easy to strip – the surface (plus its paint) can simply be peeled off dry, just like any other vinyl.

Lincrusta is an old-fashioned relief wallcovering made from linseed oil and fillers hardened like putty and formed into thin sheets. It comes in a wide range of heavily-embossed decorative effects, is hung with special adhesive and needs overpainting with gloss or eggshell paint. It is extremely durable, but once up it is difficult to remove.

Wallcoverings to Wear Well

If you want your wallcoverings to cope with steam, water splashes, sticky fingers and the like, you need a surface that is easy to keep clean. Painted wallcoverings can be sponged down, of course, but having a wallcovering with a plastic surface makes it more stain-resistant and easier to keep clean.

Washable wallpaper is a printed paper which has been given a thin clear plastic coating over the top to make it water and stain-resistant. This means it can be sponged down, but you should not use any sort of abrasive cleaner or try to scrub the surface. It is a good choice for rooms that get moderate wear, but can be difficult to remove when redecorating.

Vinyl wallcoverings differ from washable wallpapers in that the design is actually printed onto (and fused into) a plastic film, which is then paper-backed to make it easy to hang. Consequently they are much tougher than washables, and can

Fig 8 (*above*)
Wallcoverings are chosen mainly for their looks, but performance is important too. It pays to get to know what individual types can offer in this respect.

actually be scrubbed if necessary. Their other big advantage is that they are easy to strip, since the vinyl layer can be peeled off dry.

'Tile-on-a-roll' and similar foamed vinyl wallcoverings have a much thicker plastic film than ordinary vinyls, since the plastic is aerated. The surface can be heavily textured, or embossed to resemble materials such as tiles and woodgrains. They are useful in rooms prone to light condensation, since the foam surface is a moderate insulator.

Novamura is an all-plastic wall-covering, consisting of foamed polythene carrying a printed design and occasionally a light surface texture. It is also unusual in that it is hung direct from the roll – you paste the wall, not the wallcovering. It can be washed, but can tear if subjected to knocks and scuffing.

Wallcoverings to Look At

If you're not worried about how well your wallcoverings will wear or cope with dampness and condensation, you can choose purely on looks and price.

Printed wallpaper is just that – wall-paper with a printed design which may also be embossed. You can usually sponge the surface lightly to remove marks – check on the label before you hang it. It is easy to hang and strip, and so is an ideal choice if you redecorate regularly.

Flock wallpaper is printed wallpaper or paper-backed vinyl with parts of the design consisting of a raised fibre pile – usually fine wool or silk on paper types, and synthetic fibres on vinyls. The latter are very tough and hardwearing, but paper types are fairly fragile and need careful hanging to keep paste off the pile.

Paper-backed fabrics are exactly what their name implies; fabrics such as hessian, silk, tweeds and woolstrands stuck to a paper backing. Similar products include exotica like grasscloth and suede wall-coverings. Hessian is available in a range of dyed colours, or *au naturel* which is intended to be overpainted, and comes in standard-sized rolls. The others can be very expensive, and are usually sold by the metre for decorating or highlighting small areas such as alcoves or chimney breasts. They need great care in hanging, and must generally be vacuum-cleaned regularly to remove dust.

Ceramic Tiles

Ceramic tiles are thin slabs of clay decor-ated on one side with coloured glazes, often with a printed or hand-painted pat-tern too. They offer a unique combination of properties when used to decorate wall (and floor) surfaces in the home, and come in a huge range of colours and designs. They are easy to handle, fixing is simple and the resulting surface is waterproof, easy to clean and immensely hard-wearing. Their only drawback is their price.

Tiles for Walls

Tiles for use on walls are generally about 4mm (⅛in) thick, and come in a number of regular sizes. The most popular size used to be the 108mm (4¼in) square tile, still available in a limited number of ranges but displaced from the No. 1 posi-tion by larger 152mm (6in) square tiles, which are quicker to fix.

Rectangular tiles are becoming more popular too, perhaps because of the growth in continental holidays and the resulting exposure to foreign tile ranges; common sizes are 200 × 100mm (8 × 4in) and 200 × 150mm (8 × 6in). You can also buy tiles in interlocking shapes – hexagons, curved 'provençal' styles and so on. Some ranges include tile 'slips' – slim tiles 150mm (6in) long and 25mm (1in) wide, which can be used to create coloured stripes or narrow borders to tiled areas.

The range of patterns available is enor-mous, with many ranges including co-ordinated plain and patterned tiles – the

Fig 9 (*below*) There is probably more choice in ceramic tiles than in any other decorating material.

Raw Materials

latter often in the form of four or six-tile sets which are combined to make up a larger motif. Since colours can vary slight ly, it's important to buy all the tiles you need at once to ensure that they are from the same batch; it's also a good idea to unpack and mix them before fixing them to even out any colour variations.

The other important point to remember about wall tiles is that spacer lugs are no more, and the old-fashioned types rounded on one (RE) or two (REX) edges used to finish off the perimeter of half-tiled areas have virtually disappeared too. Nowadays, most tiles have square edges; these are sometimes glazed on one or two edges, sometimes not, so if you want an exposed glazed edge you must check the actual tiles before you buy. Otherwise, you'll have to use some form of edge trim. Tiles glazed on all four edges are described as 'universal'.

Tiles for Floors

Ceramic floor tiles are thicker than wall tiles – usually measuring 6mm (¼in) rather than 4mm (⅛in) thick – and are fired for longer, so they're tougher (and harder to cut). They may be glazed, with plain colour or a printed design, or un-glazed – more commonly known as quarry tiles – and many have textured surfaces to make them less slippery underfoot. Most are square-edged, so spacers have to be used to guarantee an even grouting gap; some ranges (especially quarries) still include RE and REX tiles for finishing off part-tiled areas or forming tiled skirt-ings.

Common sizes are 150mm (6in) sq, 200 x 100mm (8 x 4in) and 200mm (8in) sq; interlocking shapes are also available.

Mosaics

Mosaics are just tiny tiles – usually plain in colour, sometimes with a pattern – which are sold made up in sheets on a tough fabric backing. They are laid just like tiles in a bed of adhesive, and the gaps are grouted afterwards. Square mo-saics are the most common, but discs, hexagons and other interlocking shapes are also available. Sheets are usually 300mm (12in) sq. Note that wall and floor types are of different thicknesses.

Other Floor Tiles

Apart from ceramic tiles, three other types of tile floor covering are popular in the home, not only for their looks but because they are all very easy to lay.

Vinyl Tiles

Vinyl tiles are squares of solid or printed plastic, with either a smooth or embossed surface, and provide a very hardwearing floor covering. Cheaper types are plain, often with a veined colour effect, while more expensive types can imitate other floor coverings such as ceramic tiles, par-quet, bricks or mosaic tiles.

They have to be stuck to the floor surface – directly to concrete, to a hardboard underlay on suspended timber floors; some are self-adhesive, making them par-ticularly quick and clean to lay. The commonest tile size is 300mm (12in) sq, but other sizes are available especially in the more expensive ranges.

Cork Tiles

Cork tiles are thin slices cut from blocks of compressed cork bark, and form a floor-covering that has excellent insulating properties and also feels warm underfoot. They are made in several shades, and the cork may be stained or printed during manufacture. More expensive types have a clear vinyl surface layer to protect the cork; cheaper types have to be finished with clear sealer after laying.

Cork tiles have to be stuck to the floor surface, usually with contact adhesive. The commonest tile size is 300mm (12in) sq, although other sizes are available; most are around 6mm (¼in) thick.

Carpet Tiles

Carpet tiles are squares of carpet of various types, designed to be loose-laid. Some have a short looped or cropped pile, others a longer shag pile. Their main advantage is that they are easy to lay (and to rotate to even out wear). Set against that is their tendency to creep and ruck up in heavy traffic areas or when furniture is moved over them. They come in a range of sizes; 450, 500 and 600mm (18, 20 and 24in) squares are the commonest.

Fig 10 (*above*) Vinyl and cork floor tiles offer a wide choice of finishes and excellent durability.

Sheet Floorcoverings

The two types of sheet floorcovering most widely used in the home are sheet vinyl, mainly laid in kitchens and bathrooms, and carpet, often fitted everywhere else.

Carpet

Carpet is manufactured in an enormous range of plain colours and in geometric, abstract and floral designs. Traditionally woven carpets such as Wilton and Axminster tend to be more expensive than tufted types, and mixes containing natural fibre cost more (and generally wear better) than purely synthetic types.

Carpet is sold by the linear yard or metre from rolls 910mm (3ft) wide for 'body' carpet – ideal for staircases – or from rolls 4m (13ft) wide for broadloom – the type fitted in most other rooms.

Carpet is graded according to its durability, so it is important to choose a grade suitable for the wear the carpet can expect to get.

Sheet Vinyl

Sheet vinyl is the modern successor to old-fashioned linoleum, and comes in a huge range of colours and patterns. Cheaper types are solid, while more expensive foam-backed ones have a cushioned underside formed by incorporating small air bubbles during manufacture which makes them warmer and more resilient underfoot. It can be laid over concrete or timber floors.

Sheet vinyl is sold by the linear yard or metre (3ft 3in) from rolls in standard widths or 2, 3 and 4m (6ft 6in, 10ft and 13ft).

Timber Floors

Decorative timber floor finishes are available in two main types. The first is in the form of tiles made up by sticking fingers of wood to a strong fabric backing. The panels are usually 300 or 450mm (12 or 18in) sq., and can be stuck down or loose-laid. Most are pre-sealed.

The second is in the form of planks with tongued-and-grooved edges, designed to interlock to form a new floor surface. The planks may be solid or laminated, come in various sizes and may be pinned down or clipped together.

Fig 11 (*top*) Carpet is the most popular choice for living rooms.

Fig 12 (*above*) Sheet vinyl is ideal for rooms such as kitchens and bathrooms.

Fig 13 (*left*) Timber floors add a touch of class to any room in the house.

Tools and Equipment

Painting Equipment

Most people automatically reach for a paint brush at decorating time, and it is certainly the most popular tool for applying paint to all surfaces. However, you can also use a paint roller or a paint pad, or spray on the paint.

Paint brushes generally consist of natural animal bristle, held in a metal ferrule that is fixed to a wooden or plastic handle. There are brushes with synthetic fibre 'bristles', but they are really only suitable for rough work; the fibres do not hold paint as well as natural bristle, and lack the natural 'split ends' that help apply the paint smoothly and evenly.

Brushes come in a range of sizes, from 12mm (½in) wide up to 100 or even 150mm (4 to 6in). Basically, you choose the width to suit the job; a narrow brush for fiddly work such as painting glazing bars on windows, a broad one for flat uninterrupted surfaces such as walls or flush doors. Generally speaking, the bigger the brush the quicker you get on, but a wide brush can be very tiring to use, especially with solvent-based paints. Experiment to find what suits you best.

When choosing brushes, it pays to buy the best you can afford and to look after them well; cheap brushes give a poor finish because they contain short, cheap bristles and not very many of them!

Paint rollers are mainly used for decorating walls and ceilings using emulsion paint, where they can be run over a surface that is comparatively free of obstructions (although you will still have to use a brush to do edges, corners and fiddly bits). What you get is a roller cage and handle, onto which you slip the sleeve that actually applies the paint. Most are about 180mm (7in) wide, but you can use larger ones if you are prepared for the extra effort involved in 'driving' them. You also need a special roller tray into which to pour your paint so you can load the roller, unless you are using solid emulsion which comes in its own tray.

The cheapest sleeves are just cylinders of plastic foam; avoid using these if possible, because they absorb a lot of paint which will not come out again, are splashy to use and also very difficult to clean afterwards. Fibre sleeves come in two main types – natural and synthetic – and have short, medium or long pile. Fibre

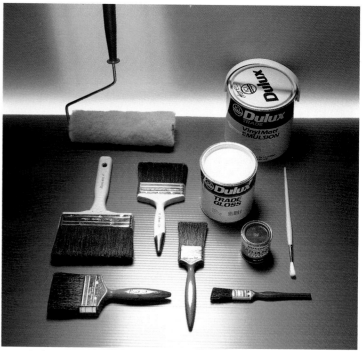

type is less important than choosing the right pile length – short for flat surfaces, medium for anything with a slight surface texture and long for heavily embossed surfaces. Be prepared for some lengthy cleaning-up work with long-pile types.

Paint pads consist of pieces of short-pile fabric stuck to a foam backing pad and attached to a metal or plastic handle. To use them, you dip the pad in the paint (poured into a shallow container or a special tray) and then draw it across the surface you are decorating. They tend to put on a thinner film than either a brush or a roller and to give a finish less good with solvent-based paints than a brush.

Spray-painting is worth considering as an alternative to hand painting in certain circumstances. However, you will need to hire or buy a spray gun and be prepared for extensive masking-off of surfaces you do not want to get paint on before you start using the gun. It is probably worth thinking about if you are decorating a house from top to bottom and can clear each room completely ready for painting, or want to paint the outside walls of your house quickly and with less effort than is involved in using a brush or roller.

You can spray paint on a small scale with an aerosol paint – ideal on fiddly jobs like painting wicker for example.

Fig 14 (*above*) You will need brushes in a range of different sizes to tackle the many painting jobs around the house, while a paint roller can speed up the decorating on large flat areas such as walls and ceilings.

Tools and Equipment

Paper-hanging Equipment

There are three main operations involved in hanging any wallcovering: pasting, hanging and trimming. To get good results at each stage you need the right equipment.

Pasting is the first stage, once you have measured and cut the wallcovering to the length you need. In the vast majority of cases you will be brushing made-up packet paste onto the length, so you will need a clean bucket to hold the paste, something to mix it with (a piece of scrap wood will do) and a brush to apply it to the wallcovering. It is best to use a 75 or 100mm (3 or 4in) wide paint brush for the job, and it is a good idea to tie a length of string across the bucket between the handle pivots so you can rest the brush on it.

You will also need a long, flat surface on which to lay the paper while you paste it, and there is no substitute for a proper pasting table. This is a simple fold-down construction, made from hardboard (or plywood on the more expensive types) fixed to a softwood frame. It measures about 1.8m (6ft) long when open, and is about 560mm (22in) wide - just wider than a standard roll of wallpaper. The legs may be of timber or lightweight metal, and fold up inside the top when the table is closed up for storage.

If you are using a ready-pasted wallcovering, the only equipment you will need is a soaking trough, usually made from polystyrene, into which to immerse the rolled-up lengths of wallcovering prior to hanging them. You can plant bulbs in it and put it on your window sill when you have finished paperhanging!

Hanging comes next. For most wallcoverings you need a special paper-hanging brush. This is a wide, long-bristled brush with a slim handle; common widths range from 190mm (7½in) up to 250mm (10in). The soft bristles not only help to follow the contours of the surface behind the wallcovering, ensuring a good bond; they also eliminate hand contact which might mark its surface.

If you are hanging washable or vinyl wallcoverings, especially ready-pasted types, you can use a sponge instead. The plastic surface layer stops you marking the wallcovering, and with ready-pasted materials the sponge helps absorb water on the surface as you hang the length.

With heavy speciality wallcoverings

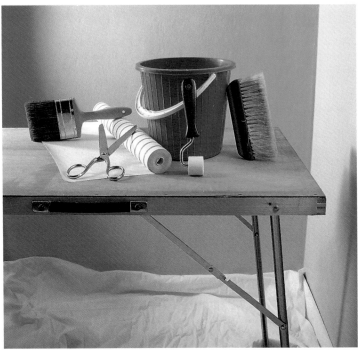

such as hessian, you may prefer to use a paint roller to bond the material securely to the wall once it is hung in place.

A seam roller is useful for ensuring that seams are well stuck down. It has a small hardwood or plastic roller running on an axle attached to a short handle, and is run along the seam after hanging and trimming are complete. It should not be used on embossed or relief wallcoverings since the embossing will be flattened.

You will need one other piece of equipment to ensure that your lengths are hung vertically: a plumb bob and line. You can of course improvize this with a length of string tied to an old nut or similar weight. You will also need a pencil and straightedge to mark the vertical line on the wall.

Trimming is the final stage of the operation, and the best tool for trimming wallcoverings is a pair of paper-hanger's scissors. The curved tips of the blades are used to press the ends of the length into the angles between the wall and the ceiling, skirting board, door or window frame, so marking the cutting line. The long blades make it easy to achieve a straight cut; sizes range up to 300mm (12in) long.

Fig 15 (*above*) A basic paper-hanging toolkit includes a pasting brush, a bucket for the paste, decorator's scissors for cutting and trimming, a paper-hanging brush and a seam roller.

Tools and Equipment

Tiling Equipment

You need very little in the way of specialist equipment for fixing tiles, just the standard measuring, marking and cutting tools you are already likely to have in your toolkit. The one exception is when you are using ceramic tiles; for these you will need a tile cutter to cut border pieces. This can be a simple 'pencil' cutter with a hardened tip, or a cutting jig with a hardened cutting wheel. The former is fine for wall tiles, but with thicker floor tiles you will find the cutting power of a jig a big help. Jigs are also more accurate than hand-held cutters.

You will also need an adhesive spreader for all ceramic and some floor tiles; this is usually supplied with the adhesive, or you can buy one separately.

For cutting awkward shapes in ceramic tiles, you can use a tile saw, a pair of pincers (to nibble away the waste area) or an ingenious power tool called the Powerfile. This drives a narrow abrasive belt round a guide bar (see Fig 17).

Flooring Equipment

As with tiling, you will need only basic hand tools – measuring tapes, a sharp handyman's knife and so on – to lay most floorcoverings. However, for laying carpet you can hire specialist tools such as a knee kicker, carpet shears and staple guns to help you make a professional job. You will also need gripper strips to secure the carpet round the room perimeter and threshold strips for room doorways.

Fig 18 (*below*) You can hire a range of professional tools to help you get good results when laying carpets.

Equipment for Preparation

You will need a range of tools and materials for preparing surfaces. For stripping paint you will need paint stripper, a blowlamp or hot air gun, a stripping knife and shavehook. For stripping wallcoverings you will need a scraper as well as, for some jobs, a hired steam wallpaper stripper. For removing tiles you will need an old chisel or a brick bolster and club hammer (for ceramic tiles). You will also need abrasives for smoothing surfaces, plus a range of fillers and mastics for making repairs.

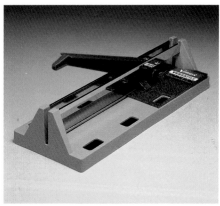

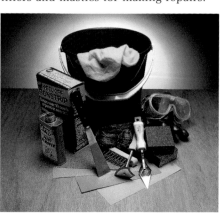

Fig 16 (*left*) A tile cutting jig is an invaluable aid, especially when working with thicker floor tiles.

Fig 17 (*below left*) A Powerfile can make light work of trimming tiles to awkward shapes.

Fig 19 (*left*) For preparing surfaces you will need a range of materials, including scrapers, strippers, filling knives, abrasives and plenty of soap and water. Gloves and goggles help protect hands and eyes from dust and dangerous liquids.

You are likely to need quite a range of different materials to carry out the sorts of decorating projects and repairs covered in this book. Where you shop for them depends on the scale and nature of the job. Here are the places to try.

Local DIY Shops

The typical independent high street DIY shop usually stocks a basic range of decorating tools and equipment, as well as small quantities of paint, primers, adhesives and the like. You will probably be offered a choice of just one or two brands. Very few stock any wallcoverings, tiles or flooring materials.

Verdict Fine for small jobs if the shop has what you need and the convenience outweighs the disadvantage of highish prices. Generally good at offering advice.

DIY Superstores

The major national chains all offer an excellent range of tools and materials for decorating projects of all types. You will find a full range of paint and related products, often with the store's own brand paint alongside one or two major national brands. Most offer several different wallcovering collections, a huge choice in wall tiles and a wide range of different floorcoverings.

They are also strong on decorating tools and accessories, plus all the sundries you will need, usually with several brands to choose from.

Verdict Excellent range of relevant products, usually at average-to-keen prices (especially for paint), but unlikely to offer much in the way of technical advice. Many open late in the evenings, and some on Sundays. Some will deliver bulky goods and will also hire equipment.

Decorators' Merchants

The obvious place to go if you want large quantities of paint, wallpaper, tiles and other materials, although many of the products they stock will be in trade rather than retail ranges. Apart from run-of-the-mill products, they will also stock or order the more exotic wallcoverings. Many also stock tools and decorating sundries.

Verdict Generally keen for decorating products, especially for large-scale pro-

jects, but only average for other materials and tools. A good source of specialist technical advice. Not open at weekends.

Builders' Timber Merchants

A good source of supply for large quantities of things like paint, varnish, woodstains and preservatives, plus in some cases ceramic tiles and floorcoverings. They will also stock most of the decorating tools and equipment you will need. Some have 'retail' counters designed to cater for the non-trade customer.

Verdict Reasonable selection of goods at average prices, although things may seem expensive since they generally stock only professional-quality products. Good for large projects. Not open at weekends.

Paint/Wallpaper Specialists

The best source of exotic wallcoverings and specialist paints, varnishes, stains and the like. Wallcoverings are usually available only to order from pattern books, so allow plenty of time for delivery.

Verdict Fine if you can find the product you want, and good for technical advice. Prices vary widely.

Flooring Superstores

These offer the widest choice in floorcoverings, especially as far as carpet and sheet vinyl are concerned. Some also stock vinyl and carpet tiles, but rarely ceramic or timber products. All usually offer a delivery service and so-called 'free' fitting included in the price; if you plan to lay your own materials do not be afraid to ask for a discount.

Verdict Generally the widest choice in sheet materials at keen-to-average prices (especially at sale times). Often open late and at weekends.

Department Stores

Some department stores have a DIY department which may stock a restricted range of paint and wallcoverings as well as decorating tools and sundries. They may also have a separate flooring department.

Verdict Generally average prices for what they stock. Some open late in the evening on weekdays, and all will generally deliver bulky items.

SAFETY

Decorating may not seem like a dangerous pastime, but there are several potential traps for the unwary.

● **Access equipment** Falls from ladders and steps cause more injuries than any other do-it-yourself activity, and there is plenty of scope for accidents when you are decorating. Always set ladders up correctly (*see* page 36) and do not try to overreach when working from them. Make sure steps are standing level and are fully extended, with any locking devices properly used. Always watch your footing when ascending or descending ladders and steps.

● **Solvents** Some paints, varnishes, adhesives and strippers give off unpleasant fumes, which can also be noxious or inflammable. Always read labels carefully when using them, and observe any safety advice given, especially as far as good ventilation of the work area is concerned.

● **Blowlamps and heat guns** Always take care when stripping paint with these tools. In particular, avoid pointing the flame or air stream at anything inflammable, and take care to dispose of hot scrapings safely.

Using a Paintbrush

Paintbrushes are by far the most widely used decorating tools. Many people prefer them to rollers for painting walls and ceilings (and you still need a brush to touch in the edges even if you do use a roller), and paint pads remain very much a minority taste.

You can treat paintbrushes in one of two ways. The first is to buy the cheapest brush you can find and simply throw it away when you have finished with it, while the second is to buy the best quality brush you can afford and then to look after it carefully so that it gives years of service. The latter course is the better one to adopt, because it will give you far better results and will encourage far more pride in doing a good job. An expensive brush has longer, better-quality bristles (and many more of them) than a cheap brush, which will tend to shed bristles all over your fresh paintwork and will not hold much paint or give a good finish. So long as you clean it thoroughly after every job and store it properly (see Tip), it will last a surprisingly long time.

What to do

If you are using a new brush for the first time, brush its bristles backwards and forwards across the palm of your hand to dislodge any loose bristles and dust. Then pour some paint into your paint kettle, through a strainer made from nylon tights or similar fabric to catch any bits if you are working from a partly-used tin.

Dip the brush into the paint to about one third of the bristle length, and draw the sides of the bristles lightly against the thin string tied across the kettle to remove excess paint which might cause runs or drips. Then apply the paint to the surface you are decorating in a series of parallel strokes, each slightly overlapping its neighbour. Work along the grain direction if you are painting wood.

Brush the paint out with strokes at right angles to the initial ones, then finish off with more strokes in the original direction. Repeat the process to paint the next area, blending the two together with more light brush strokes.

What you need:
- paint brush
- paint kettle
- strainer (e.g. nylon from tights)
- wire or string

CHECK
- that the ferrule of a previously-used brush is free from rust, which could discolour the paint. If you find any, throw the brush away.

TIP
Wrap wet brushes in kitchen foil or food wrap if you have to stop painting for a while. This will stop the paint from drying on the bristles.

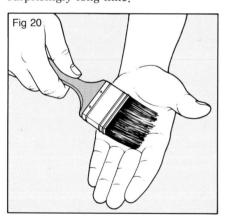

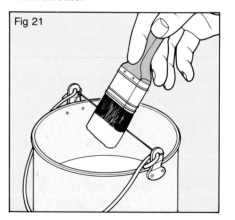

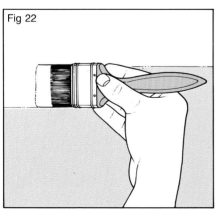

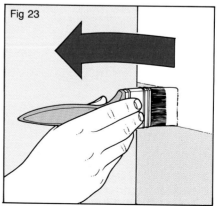

Fig 20 Before using a new brush, work it backwards and forwards against your hand to remove dust and loose bristles.

Fig 21 Load the brush to no more than half the bristle length, and remove excess paint on a string tied across your paint kettle.

Fig 22 Apply the paint first in parallel bands, then brush these gently together with transverse strokes before finishing off by brushing in the original direction.

Fig 23 At corners, brush towards the edge to avoid a paint build-up on the external angle.

Using Paint Rollers and Pads

Paint rollers with their detachable sleeves are ideal for applying paint quickly to large areas. Professional decorators use them to apply gloss and other solvent-based paints as well as for emulsion, but most amateur decorators use them mainly for putting emulsion onto walls and ceilings, preferring brushes or pads for painting woodwork. Apart from the speed of application, rollers are better than brushes or pads at coping with textured and embossed surfaces, both of which are popular for walls and ceilings.

DIY paint rollers take sleeves 180mm (7in) or 230mm (9in) wide, and a variety of synthetic and natural fibre sleeves are available. Generally speaking, synthetic fibre sleeves work best with emulsion paints; the more textured the surface, the longer the fabric pile should be.

Paint pads have a piece of short-pile fabric stuck to a plastic or metal handle, and come in a range of sizes for painting woodwork as well as walls and ceilings. Large pads often have small edge wheels to guide the pad in wall-ceiling angles.

What to do

If you are using a roller, first select the correct sleeve for the surface you are painting. Then strain some paint into your roller tray, filling it to a depth of about 19mm (¾in), and load your roller evenly by running it down the tray's slope into the paint and back again several times. If you are using 'solid' emulsion, simply run the roller backwards and forwards over the paint surface to load the sleeve.

Apply the paint by rolling first in one direction, then at right angles, to ensure even coverage of the surface. Re-load the roller as necessary and paint the next area, blending it in with the first as you work across the surface.

Load a small paint pad by dipping it lightly into the paint, then 'stroke' the paint onto the surface. With larger pads, use a special tray with a grooved roller that loads the pad evenly as it is drawn over the roller. As with rollers, apply the paint with strokes in one direction, then go over them with strokes at right angles.

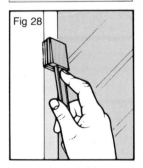

Fig 28 (*above*)   Use a small pad for narrow surfaces such as glazing bars.

Fig 24

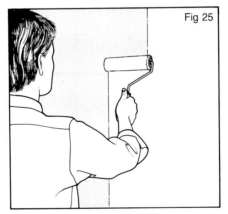

Fig 25

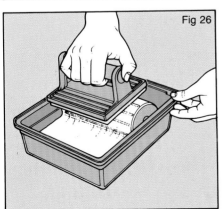

Fig 26

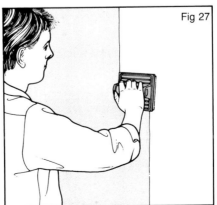

Fig 27

Fig 24   Pour some paint into your roller tray, and load the roller evenly by running it up and down the slope.

Fig 25   Apply the paint in even parallel bands, then work the roller backwards and forwards across the area to get even coverage.

Fig 26   Load a large paint pad using a special roller tray. Dip small pads straight into the paint.

Fig 27   Draw the pad across the surface to squeeze out the paint.

Cutting and Pasting Wallpaper

It is wise to choose a wallcovering with a straight pattern match (see page 11) for your first attempts at paper-hanging, so you can concentrate on practising your technique without having an additional complicating factor to worry about. Make sure you have bought enough rolls to complete the job (see page 89), and that their labels all carry the same batch number so you can be confident there will be no slight colour variations between individual rolls.

Read the instructions on the label to find out what type of paste should be used to hang it, and buy a packet that will make up enough paste for the number of rolls you are hanging. The smallest packets will hang 3 or 4 rolls, while larger packets cater for up to 10 or 12 rolls. If you are hanging washable or vinyl papers, make sure the paste contains a fungicide. Ready-mixed tub pastes cover roughly 3 rolls per litre. If you are hanging a ready-pasted wallcovering, remember to buy a polystyrene water tray in which to soak the individual lengths.

What to do

Set up your pasting table and mix up some paste, stirring it continuously as you add the powder to stop lumps forming. Then measure the wall height or ceiling width, add about 100mm (4in) to allow for trimming at each end, and cut the first length. If you are hanging a paper with a straight pattern match on a ceiling or a wall with no major obstacles, you can then use the first length as a guide to cutting several more to the same length.

Lay the first length on the table, using a ruler or a timber batten to stop it rolling up, and brush paste generously up the centre of the length. Slide it over so one edge aligns with the far edge of the table, and brush paste out towards that edge. Then slide it towards the near edge of the table and repeat the process.

When you have pasted the first part of the length, fold the pasted area over on itself and slide the length along the table so you can paste the rest of the length. Fold that over too, ready for hanging.

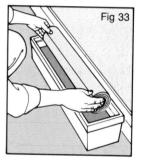

Fig 33 (*above*) Roll ready-pasted papers loosely, top end outermost, and immerse them in a trough of cold water for the recommended time.

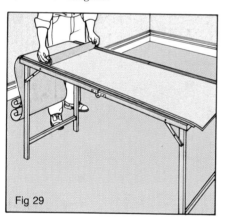

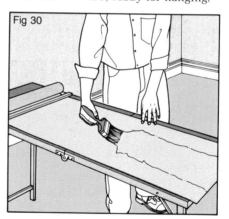

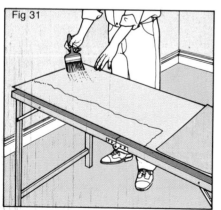

Fig 29 Cut several lengths and lay them face down on your pasting table.

Fig 30 Start applying paste to the central area of the first length.

Fig 31 Align one edge of the paper with the edge of the table and paste it. Repeat for the other edge.

Fig 32 Fold the paper paste side to paste side, ready for carrying to the wall.

Hanging the First Lengths

With many types of wallcovering, the paper stretches slightly as it absorbs moisture from the paste. For this reason, the paper manufacturer will recommend that the pasted paper is left to soak for a few minutes before it is hung, and it is vital to follow this advice; if you do not, you will find it impossible to get an accurate pattern match between adjacent lengths. As your paper-hanging technique improves, you will find it possible to speed up the work by pasting one length, then pasting a second while the first soaks. You then hang the first while the second soaks, paste a third, hang the second and so on. Alternatively, get a helper to paste lengths while you hang them. If you are working on your own, it is a good idea to use a kitchen timer to remind you not to allow lengths to over-soak.

Before you paste any lengths, make sure you have suitable access equipment set up. For papering walls a hop-up or a pair of short steps is ideal, since you can quickly move it out of the way when you have hung the top end of a length.

What to do

You must always hang the first length of paper on any wall to a plumbed vertical line; you can never trust walls to be perfectly true or corners to be perfectly vertical. Draw this on the wall just less than the roll width away from the corner.

Carry your pasted and folded length to the wall and climb your steps. Supporting the pasted length over one arm, unfold the top end of the length and slide it into place on the wall with an overlap of about 50mm (2in) at the ceiling angle. Align one edge of the paper with the plumbed line and allow the rest of the length to unfold down the wall so you can align the whole length of the edge with the line.

Then use a paper-hanging brush to smooth the paper onto the wall, working from the top downwards and the centre outwards to brush out air bubbles. Crease the overlap at the ceiling and skirting board with the blade of your scissors, cut off the excess and brush the ends back into place. Repeat for the next length.

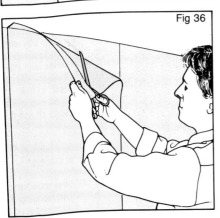

Fig 34 Always hang the first length on each wall to a plumbed line. Support the folded paper with one hand while you align the top part of the length with the line.

Fig 35 Allow the rest of the length to unfold down the wall, and brush it into place. Work from the top downwards and from the centre towards the edges.

Fig 36 Use your scissors to mark the paper in the wall/ceiling angle, then trim it to length and brush it back into place. Repeat at the skirting, then hang the next length beside the first.

Fig 37 Except on embossed papers, run a seam roller down the seams to ensure good adhesion to the wall.

Setting out Small Tiled Areas

The joints between ceramic tiles are a strong visual feature, since the individual tiles are relatively small. It is therefore important to devote some time to planning where the joints will fall on any area of tiling, large or small, for two reasons. The first is to try to achieve an element of symmetry, especially where the tiling is above a feature such as a washbasin, or is covering an area of wall between two windows. The second is to try to avoid having to cut very thin strips of tile to fit into corners – difficult to do successfully, and likely to look odd as well.

On small tiled areas such as splashbacks behind sinks, basins and baths, it is relatively simple to use the actual tiles you will be fixing to plan how the tiles will be positioned to the wall. With a free-standing feature the tiles should generally be centred visually on the feature, whereas with a bath splashback where the tiling will be on two adjacent walls any cut tiles generally look best when placed at the internal corner where the two areas of tiling meet.

What to do

Above a sink or basin, start by marking the centre line of the appliance on the wall behind it. Then stand tiles in place against the wall on either side of the line, adding more tiles so you can see what width of cut tile (if any) will be needed to complete the row at each end. Ideally cut tiles should be avoided on a small area like this; it's better to stick to using just whole tiles, even if this means the splashback will be slightly wider or narrower than the appliance. If cut pieces cannot be avoided and your layout means these will be less than about a quarter of the tile width, try the alternative arrangement of placing the first tile on the centre line; this will result in wider cut pieces at each end of the rows.

Above a bath, place whole tiles at the outer corners of the bath and then add others back towards the internal corner so you can see how wide the cut pieces will be. If they look like being impossibly narrow, move the starter tiles in or out.

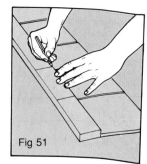

Fig 51

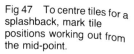

Fig 51 (*above*) Mark tile widths on a timber straightedge and use this as a tile gauge to see where cut tiles will fall.

Fig 47 To centre tiles for a splashback, mark tile positions working out from the mid-point.

Fig 48 If this will result in very narrow cut pieces at each side, centre the first tile on the mid-point instead of alongside it.

Fig 49 For very small areas, try to use only whole tiles for a balanced appearance.

Fig 50 When tiling behind a bath, place whole tiles at the outer edges of the area and cut tiles in the corner.

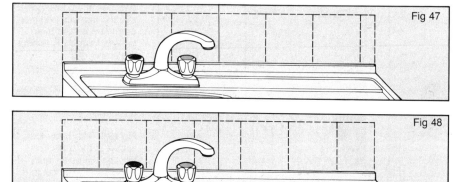

Fig 47

Fig 48

Fig 49

Fig 50

Setting out Tiled Walls

If you plan to tile a whole wall – or even a whole room – the question of accurate setting-out assumes even greater importance than when you are tiling a small area. Not only do you want to achieve the same element of symmetry on each wall and avoid having very narrow pieces of cut tile; you also have to ensure that the tiles are fixed to a true horizontal and vertical grid to ensure that the joints are aligned accurately in both directions across the wall surface. This calls for some careful planning and, in many situations, a fair degree of compromise.

What to do

If you are tiling just one wall that contains no obstacles such as door or window openings, your aim is to centre the tiles horizontally and vertically with cut pieces of equal size at each end of the rows and columns. Make up a gauging rod by marking tile widths on it (see Fig 51 on page 26), and mark horizontal and vertical lines on the wall to indicate the centre in each direction. Then hold your gauging rod against the wall to see how wide the cut pieces will be at each end of the rows and columns. Adjust your starting position if necessary, as for tiling small areas.

Where the wall has a major feature such as a window opening, it is generally better to centre the tiling on this rather than on the wall as a whole since it will be the visual centre of attention. Start at the centre line of the window and see how tiles will fall at the edges of the window reveal, again adjusting your starting point if necessary to get the best arrangement.

If tiling will also be carried onto features such as bath panels, aim to have whole tiles at the external corner of the panelling and cut pieces (if required) at the internal angle between the panels and the walls.

Having established your starting points in both directions, all that remains is to pin truly horizontal timber battens to the walls being tiled to support the lowest row of whole tiles just above the skirting board. Use masonry nails for the fixings.

What you need:
● tiles
● tile adhesive
● adhesive spreader
● tiling gauge stick
● steel tape measure
● pencil

Fig 52 When tiling whole walls, use your tiling gauge to get the best compromise in centring tiles on each wall while taking account of any major obstacles such as window openings.

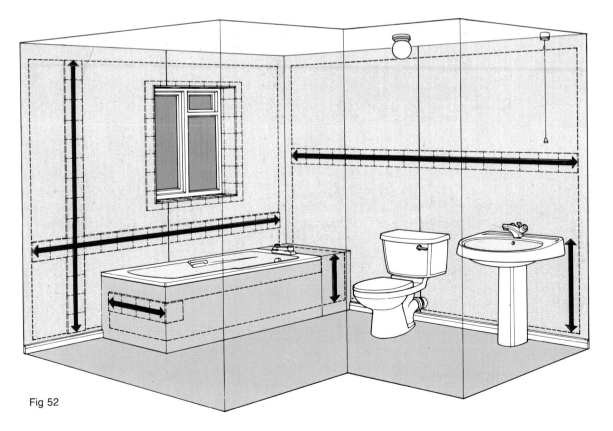

Fig 52

Fixing Whole Tiles

Once you have completed the setting-out of the area you intend to tile, you are ready to start actually fixing the tiles in place with tile adhesive. If you are tiling just a small area such as a splashback, it is safe to align the horizontal rows with the back edge of the bath, basin or sink; this is in any case likely to be set at a true horizontal, so there is no risk of the tiles being placed out of alignment. However, if you are tiling a whole wall you not only need a horizontal batten to support the lowest row of tiles. You also need a vertical guide batten at one side of the area, in line with the last column of whole tiles, to ensure that the columns are truly vertical. Pin these battens to the wall surface with masonry pins, driven only partly home so you can easily prise them out again with a claw hammer when you have finished fixing all the whole tiles and want to fill in round the wall perimeter with narrow cut-to-size pieces.

If you are tiling onto plasterboard, give the board surface a couple of coats of emulsion paint first to seal it.

What to do

For a small area such as a splashback, mark the extent of the tiling on the wall in pencil, and spread tile adhesive onto the wall with the toothed spreader supplied with the adhesive. Press the points of the teeth against the plaster to ensure that the adhesive is applied in ridges of a standard height, giving an adhesive bed of uniform thickness when the tiles are pressed into it. Then set the tiles in the bottom row into position one by one, followed by those in the second row, checking that they are aligned accurately and sit level with each other.

For a larger area, spread a band of adhesive onto the wall in the angle between your guide battens, and bed the bottom row of tiles into place across the full width of the wall. Use a timber batten across the tile faces to check that they are set flush with their neighbours. Then spread more adhesive and place more tiles, working up the wall row by row until all the whole tiles are in place.

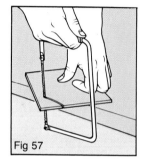

Fig 57 (*above*) Use a tile saw to make cut-outs round obstacles such as pipes.

Fig 53 Once you have worked out the best starting point, nail guide battens to the wall. Check that they are truly vertical and horizontal.

Fig 54 Spread some tile adhesive on the wall and bed the first row of whole tiles in place. Then add further rows until all the whole tiles are in place.

Fig 55 Run a knife blade between the bottom row of tiles and the support batten, then leave the adhesive to set for 24 hours.

Fig 56 Prise the battens off and cut and fit the edge tiles. Measure each one individually for a good fit.

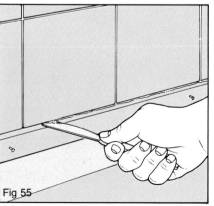

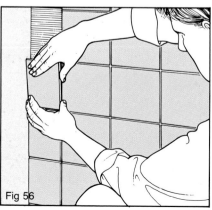

Tiling Corners and Edges

With all the whole tiles in place, your next job is to cut and place narrower pieces of tile along the perimeter of the wall. Where you are tiling adjacent walls, you will also have to fit tiles to internal and external corners. You may also have to cut tiles to fit round obstacles such as pipes passing through walls.

What to do

At internal corners, measure the width of the gap at the end of each row, mark this on the tile and cut it using your tile cutter. Spread some adhesive on its back and press it into place. Repeat this for all the other perimeter tiles.

At external corners it looks best if two whole tiles meet on the angle. You can either let the tiles on one wall overlap the edges of those on the next – fine if they have well-glazed edges – or you can use tile corner trim. This is a slim plastic beading which is bedded in the tile adhesive and provides a neat finish to the angle when the tiles are fixed in place.

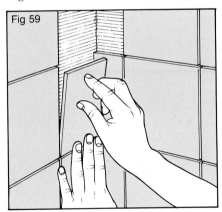

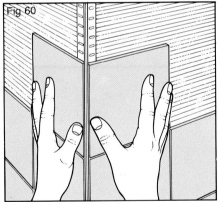

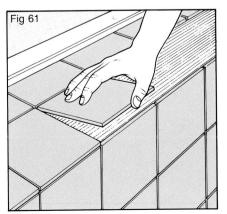

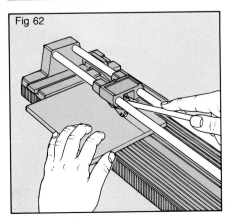

Fig 58 (*above*) As an alternative to overlapping tiles at external corners, you can use neat plastic trim strips.

Fig 59 At internal corners, leave a grouting gap between the cut pieces.

Fig 60 Always place whole tiles on either side of an external angle, with one tile overlapping the edge of the other. Alternatively, use plastic trim strips.

Fig 61 On window sills, place whole tiles so they overlap the top edges of the wall tiles and fill in with cut pieces if necessary.

Fig 62 Use a tiling jig rather than a hand-held tile cutter for accurate and easy cutting.

29

Tiling Round Doors and Windows

When you are tiling walls, the trickiest areas to deal with – as with paperhanging – are doorways and window recesses. Try to centre your tiling on the opening if this is possible and does not cause problems with extra-thin cut pieces elsewhere on the wall. This ensures that there are cut pieces of equal width at either side of the opening for a neat symmetrical effect.

What to do

With window recesses, decide first of all whether the sides of the reveal will be fully tiled. You may have an existing wooden window board, and you may prefer simply to emulsion the sides and head of the reveal. If they are to be fully tiled, decide next whether you want to use tile trim on the external angles, or whether to allow the tiles within the recess to overlap the edges of those on the face wall. Your choice will affect how you cut the tiles on the face wall, so you must make this decision before you actually fit them.

Place the edge trim if you are using it. Then cut and fit tiles round the recess on the face wall, followed by whole tiles on the sill and the reveal sides. Add cut pieces between these and the window frame if the reveal depth requires them.

Above window and door openings, use a batten to support the last row of whole tiles above the opening. When the adhesive has hardened, remove the batten and fit cut pieces to the face wall. Then finish tiling a window reveal by pressing whole and cut tiles firmly into the adhesive at the head of the reveal, using adhesive tape to provide some additional support while the adhesive sets.

Around door frames, simply mark and cut tiles to fit against the door architrave at each side and across the top, as for tiling internal corners.

To fit tiles round smaller obstacles such as light switches and power points, it is best to use a tile saw to cut the L-shaped pieces of tile needed to fit round the accessory. Use the saw to make small cut-outs for pipes and the like too.

What you need:
- tiles
- tile adhesive
- adhesive spreader
- spirit level
- timber battens
- masonry nails
- hammer
- tile cutter
- tile saw
- adhesive tape

CHECK
- that tiles on the underside of window reveals are well supported while the adhesive sets.

TIP
Use plastic tile trim for external angles if the tiles you are using have imperfectly-glazed edges.

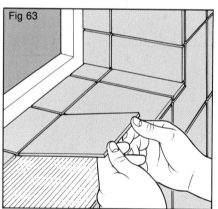

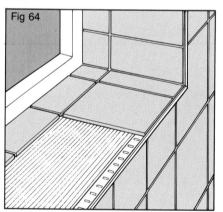

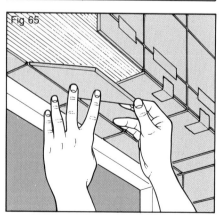

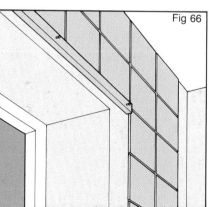

Fig 63 Tile the sides of window recesses first, then the sill.

Fig 64 Use plastic edge trim instead of overlapping the tile edges, especially if these are not glazed.

Fig 65 Use adhesive tape to give tiles additional support on the underside of window and door reveals.

Fig 66 Use a batten to support the last row of whole tiles above a window or door reveal.

Fig 67 (*right*) Use a spreader with a flexible edge to force grout into the gaps between the tiles.

Fig 68 (*right*) When the grout has dried, polish the tile surfaces with a dry cloth to remove smears.

Avoiding Decorating Defects

Once you have finished fixing whole and cut tiles to your walls, the final stage is to fill all the gaps between them – a process known as grouting. Grout is water-resistant, so apart from leaving neat horizontal and vertical joints it also prevents water from penetrating behind the tiles and weakening the adhesive – a common cause of tile failure especially in bathrooms. Grout is generally sold ready-mixed in a tub, complete with a flexible spreader. White grout is by far the most common, although coloured grout is now becoming more widely available.

What to do

Scrape any dried tile adhesive off the faces of the tiles with a stripping knife or similar tool. Then use the flexible grout spreader to force grout into the joint lines by drawing it across them at roughly right angles. Wipe off excess grout as you proceed, then leave the filled joints to harden before polishing excess grout off the tiles with a dry cloth.

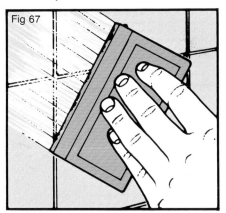

Fig 67

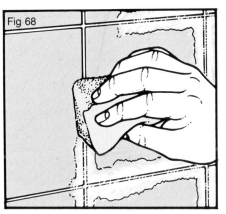

Fig 68

Many amateur decorators are disappointed with the results of their efforts, in particular as far as painting and paper-hanging are concerned. Here are some guidelines to help you avoid problems as you work, and how to put things right if they seem to be going wrong.

Painting problems One of the commonest problems involves the appearance of foreign bodies in the wet paint film. These may be dust particles already on the surface, bits blown onto the wet paint (common out of doors), bristle fragments, or debris in the paint container. Avoid this by dusting surfaces before painting, by avoiding windy days, by cleaning brushes thoroughly before starting painting, and by straining paint into a paint kettle instead of working from the tin.

A loss of gloss is often caused by surfaces being damp or very cold; avoid these conditions if you can. Patches of sheen when using eggshell paints result from over-fast drying, caused either by high room temperatures or over-porous surfaces that should have been primed.

Various faults arise if you try to paint over a previous coating that is not dry. One is the presence of heavy brush marks which will not brush out, and another is stickiness caused by the solvent in the top coat softening the coat below.

If the paint apparently fails to cover what is beneath it, avoid overbrushing and make sure you are working in good light so you can see any missed areas (called 'holidays' in the trade). If it will not dry, there may be grease or wax on the surface beneath; strip off the new paint and then thoroughly degrease the surface.

Do not try to apply too thick a coating to get good coverage. You will get runs in the wet paint film, 'fat' edges where paint collects on external angles, and wrinkling as the top of the paint film dries more quickly than the wet paint underneath.

Paper-hanging The two commonest problems are blistering and lifting seams. The former may be caused by uneven pasting, under or over-soaking, even using the wrong type of paste, and by insufficient brushing during hanging which leaves air trapped behind the wallcovering. The latter is usually the result of poor pasting leaving dry edges. Both can be cured by careful pasting and hanging techniques.

CHECK
• that surfaces you are decorating are clean, dry and free from grease or foreign matter
• that paint from part-used tins is free from bits by straining it into a kettle before use
• that wallpaper paste is free from lumps
• that adhesives are applied evenly and completely cover the surface.

Laying Floor Tiles

Several floorcovering materials come in tile form, including cork, vinyl, carpet, ceramic and quarry tiles. Their advantage over sheet materials is that the small units are easy to handle and to lay, especially in awkwardly-shaped rooms. However, they do need careful setting out if the finished result is to look neat and symmetrical, in much the same way as when you are tiling a wall.

Fortunately, setting-out is easier to handle on the floor because you can easily dry-lay tiles on the floor surface and work out the starting point that gives the neatest arrangement. Most tiles are laid to a grid parallel with the room's walls, but there is no reason why you should not experiment with diagonal arrangements instead if, you want to achieve an unusual and dramatic overall effect.

Most tiles are laid working outwards from the room's centre point towards the perimeter; the exceptions are ceramic and quarry tiles, which are usually laid from a starting point in one corner of the room using guide battens fixed to the floor.

What to do

In a regularly-shaped room, start by finding the midpoints of opposite walls and join them with string lines. The point where the lines cross give you the room's true centre.

Next, place one tile in the angle between the string lines, and dry-lay a row of tiles from here to the room's perimeter in each direction. This will allow you to see how wide a gap will be left along each wall. If this is between about a quarter and three-quarters of a tile wide you can leave the starting point unchanged, but if you will be left with either a very narrow gap or one fractionally less than a tile width you should move the starting point across the room in the appropriate direction by half a tile width.

In rooms with lots of alcoves and awkward wall angles, dry-lay a row of tiles down the centre of the room and then lay other rows out towards the walls at various points. Adjust the starting point to get the best possible compromise fit.

What you need:
- string lines and pins
- steel measuring tape
- pencil
- tiles
- timber battens
- hammer and nails

CHECK
- that your string lines are square to each other
- that you allow for a grouting space when setting out ceramic tiles.

TIP
Always set aside a couple of tiles as spares, so you will be able to repair any tiles that are damaged in the future.

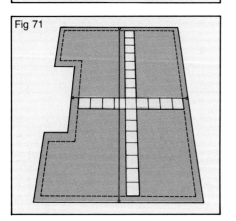

Fig 69

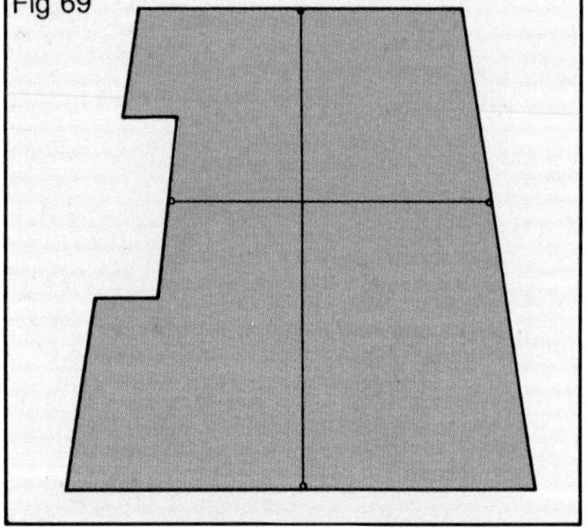

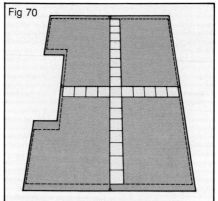

Fig 70

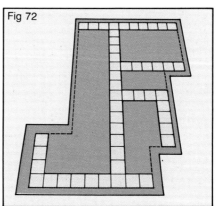

Fig 71

Fig 72

Fig 69 To find the centre point of the room, pin string lines to the mid-points of opposite walls.

Fig 70 Dry-lay rows of tiles alongside the lines towards each wall.

Fig 71 If this leaves unacceptably narrow gaps at the perimeter of the room, adjust the starting point slightly.

Fig 72 In awkwardly-shaped rooms, dry-lay rows of tiles into all the angles to get the best arrangement.

Laying Floor Tiles

If you want to lay the tiles on a diagonal format, again start by finding the room centre. Then place a tile over the centre point at 45° to the string lines, and dry-lay rows of tiles out towards the walls along the lines. Also dry-lay rows of tiles towards the room corners so you can see how close to the skirting board the last whole tiles will fall. You have two choices as far as finishing off the perimeter of the room is concerned. The first is to fill in with cut tiles all round, while the second is to lay a border of tiles parallel to the skirting boards. The latter is likely to prove less wasteful of tiles, since all the infill tiles laid on the diagonal next to the border will be exactly half tiles.

With ceramic and quarry tiles, dry-lay rows as for other types and adjust the starting point if necessary. Then draw lines on the floor in one corner of the room to indicate the edges of the last whole tiles, and pin battens to the floor to act as a guide for laying the tiles. Use masonry nails on solid floors driven partly in for ease of removal.

Fig 73 (*above*) Tiled floors offer a combination of good looks and excellent durability.

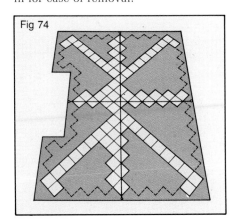

Fig 74 If you want a diagonal arrangement, again dry-lay rows of tiles outwards to check on the size of cut border pieces.

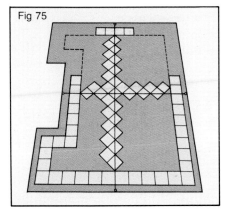

Fig 75 Alternatively, plan to have a border of tiles laid square round the diagonally-tiled central area.

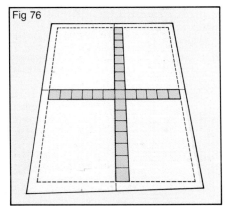

Fig 76 Once you are happy with the tile arrangement, mark the position of your starting point for whole tiles in one corner of the room.

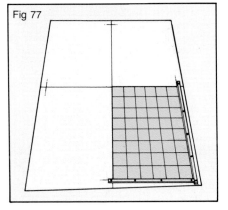

Fig 77 Fix guide battens at this corner, ready for tiling to begin.

Laying Sheet Floorcoverings

Sheet floorcoverings such as vinyl and carpet are more difficult for the amateur to lay because of the sheer size of the sheet – both materials are now sold mainly in 4m (13ft) widths, which means that most rooms can be fitted with a single piece laid without seams, but this does make for handling difficulties.

For this reason, it is probably best to confine your first attempt at laying these materials to a fairly small room with relatively few obstacles – a hallway, perhaps, for sheet vinyl, or a spare bedroom for carpet. As far as laying carpet is concerned, it is also wise to lay a cheap foam-backed carpet to begin with.

With both materials the laying principle is broadly the same. Start by cutting the sheet roughly to size – say 150mm (6in) larger than the room all round. Do this in a larger room, on the drive, or on the lawn if it is dry. The bring it into the room where it will be laid, unroll it and allow the edges to lap up the walls all round. Leave it to condition to room temperature and humidity before starting to fit it.

What to do

In a room with a chimney breast (or a similar obstacle such as a piece of built-in furniture), start by making long cuts in the edge of the floorcovering next to it so tongues of material can fall back into the alcoves. Cut off most of the waste against the face of the chimney breast.

With carpet, make diagonal cuts at the internal corners of the room next, to allow it to lie flat with the trim resting up against the skirting boards. Make similar release cuts at external corners, cutting off too little material to begin with rather than too much. Now you can start trimming the carpet to fit all round the room, using a sharp knife held with the blade pointing downwards into the angle between floor and skirting board.

With sheet vinyl, start by aligning the sheet against the longest clear wall of the room before making any release cuts. If the skirting board undulates along its length, pull the sheet away so you can scribe the wall profile onto it and trim it to

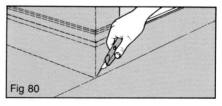

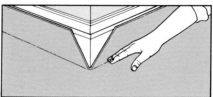

Fig 78   With sheet materials, simply unroll the sheet in the room with one edge against the longest straight wall, and make release cuts (*see below*) to allow it to fit round obstacles and into corners.

Fig 79   At internal corners make a cut across the corner at 45°, then press the sheet back ready for final edge trimming.

Fig 80   At external corners let the sheet lap up against the first wall and make a diagonal release cut upwards from the corner. Let the flap fall to the floor round the corner, then make a similar release cut there.

Laying Sheet Floorcoverings

match. Use a piece of scrap wood with a nail driven through it – more positive than a pencil, and unlikely to break – and draw the batten along the floorcovering, keeping it at right angles to the skirting. Cut along the scribed line with a sharp knife, then slide the scribed edge back up against the skirting board.

Next, make release cuts as for carpet at the other corners of the room and at obstacles, and let the trim rest up against the skirting board. Use a piece of thin board to press the vinyl down into the angle and trim it with a sharp knife.

At doorways, make a series of release cuts into the sheet to allow you to remove a little material at a time for a perfect fit. Less care is needed with carpets, since the pile will conceal any slight inaccuracies in your cutting.

In rooms without seams, stick the edges of both sheet vinyl and foam-backed carpet down with lengths of double-sided adhesive tape. Use this under seams too or, for sheet vinyl only, spread a band of flooring adhesive beneath the seam.

Fig 82

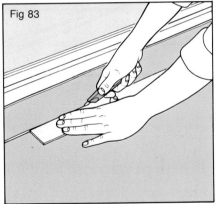

Fig 83

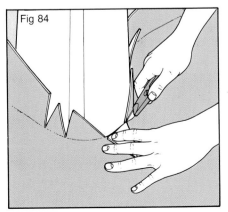

Fig 84

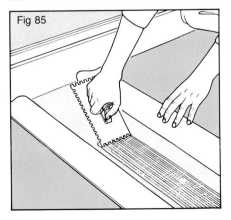

Fig 85

Fig 81 (*above*) Sheet vinyl floorcoverings are hard-wearing and can imitate a wide range of other floor surfaces.

Fig 82 To get a good fit against an uneven wall with sheet vinyl, use a nail and batten to scribe the wall outline onto the sheet.

Fig 83 Along other walls use a sharp knife and a straightedge, pressed hard into the angle, to trim off excess material.

Fig 84 Make a series of release cuts round awkward obstacles, then trim each tongue off in turn. Alternatively, use a template (*see page 58*).

Fig 85 Where seams are unavoidable, stick them down into a band of flooring adhesive, or use special double-sided adhesive tape.

Using Access Equipment

For most interior decorating jobs you will need nothing more complex than a pair of steps. However, you can make jobs such as painting walls and ceilings and putting up ceiling paper a lot easier with scaffold boards or lightweight staging (which you can hire – see page 19) set between two stepladders or trestles.

On stairwells, you need a stable high-level platform to reach the ceiling and the highest parts of the walls, and this is best improvized using sections of ladder, steps and scaffold boards. Two typical examples are shown in the illustrations below. Note the battens nailed to the stairs and landing to lock the ladders in place, and ropes and cramps to prevent the boards from slipping. Always use two boards to prevent sagging on long spans.

An alternative in stairwells is to use components of a slot-together platform tower to build a work platform on the stairs. You can use these components instead of trestles and staging too.

For outdoor decorating, a ladder is most people's first choice for painting upstairs woodwork. However, a platform tower is far safer and more comfortable to work on for long periods, and provides a safe place to store tools and materials too. It is also worth using one for painting the upper reaches of exterior walls.

What you need:
- steps
- scaffold boards
- ladder sections
- clamps or ropes
- battens
- hammer and nails

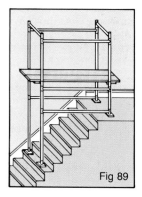

Fig 89 (*above*)   As an alternative you can hire special slot-together stair platforms.

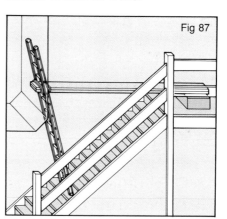

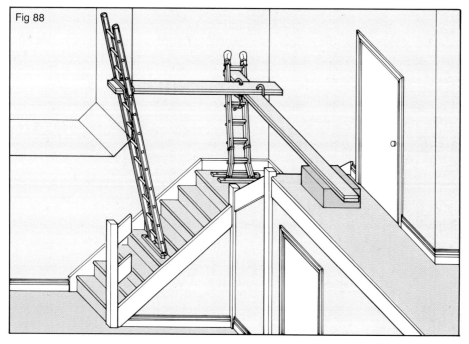

Fig 86   Use steps and scaffold boards, or trestles and staging, for painting walls and ceilings.

Fig 87   In straight stairwells, use one section of an extension ladder to support a pair of scaffold boards.

Fig 88   On dog-leg flights, combine steps, ladders, hop-ups and scaffold boards to create a working platform. Use battens to secure ladder feet on treads and landings, and rope or clamp boards together for safety.

INDOOR JOBS

As far as decorating is concerned, there is a huge range of jobs you can carry out inside the house. They range from simple tasks such as painting walls, ceilings and woodwork or hanging curtains that just about every householder carries out at some time or another, to more complex projects such as papering stairwells, fitting wall cladding or laying floorcoverings. All of the jobs covered in this chapter are well within the capabilities of the amateur decorator, and since many of them are fairly labour-intensive, carrying them out yourself will save a great deal of money compared with calling in a professional to do the work for you.

Whatever you decide to tackle, you will find the necessary materials and equipment widely available from all the regular do-it-yourself suppliers. All you need are the basic skills to do the work and the time and will to complete the job.

What You Can Tackle

You do not have to be a master decorator to carry out many of the most popular projects. Here are some examples.

Painting walls and ceilings This is without doubt the simplest of all decorating jobs, and the one that offers the biggest savings for the do-it-yourselfer since labour charges are such a major part of the overall cost. Non-drip paints, and most recently solid emulsions, have made the job child's play, and you can also experiment with textured finishes as an alternative to flat surfaces.

Painting woodwork, fixtures and fittings Doors, windows and other interior woodwork, as well as things like radiators and pipework, all need decorating too. Tackled one at a time, they do not seem such a difficult prospect, especially if you use time-savers such as combined primer-undercoats or self-undercoating gloss.

Papering a room This is probably the most daunting of indoor projects, yet with good preparation and planning you will be surprised at how quickly the lengths go up, especially if you use ready-pasted papers. Products like woodchip or embossed wallpapers can help hide wall defects too, and just need a fresh coat of paint if you fancy a change of decor.

Papering ceilings and stairwells These two jobs pose a bigger challenge, but the only major differences compared with papering the walls of a room lie in learning to handle longer lengths of paper and working off access equipment.

Putting up friezes and borders Many wallcovering manufacturers now offer co-ordinating decorative friezes and borders with their wallpaper collections, allowing you to achieve stylish and professional-looking results in any room.

Tiling a room Tackling a whole kitchen or bathroom is Mount Everest as far as tiling is concerned, yet is no more than the sum of its parts once the setting-out of each wall is done.

Cladding walls and ceilings Natural timber cladding is a popular material, and installing it requires only the barest minimum of woodworking skills.

Laying floorcoverings This is a job where many do-it-yourselfers fear to tread, while others tackle it quite happily. As a general rule it is easier to lay tiles rather than sheet materials, but even the latter can be quite manageable once you have mastered the basic skills.

Hanging curtains and blinds Adding the finishing touches to a room involves just making secure wall fixings.

Fig 90 (*above*)   Even if your decorating is as simple as applying a coat of white paint everywhere, there is nothing to beat the appearance of a freshly-decorated room.

Painting Walls and Ceilings

Painting walls and ceilings is typical of so many decorating jobs, involving the repetition of a simple operation – wielding a brush, roller or pad – over what often seems like acres of featureless terrain! Once you have mastered the technique of actually applying the paint, all you have to overcome is the boredom; painting offers the perfect opportunity to listen to the radio or to a favourite record in peace as you work.

The key to successful painting lies in good preparation. If you are redecorating over existing paint in good condition, all you will need to do is to wash the surface down with strong detergent or sugar soap first to remove dirt, grease, smokers' tar stains and the like. On painted plaster surfaces, fill cracks wider than a hairline and repair any localized damage (see page 79). Seal bare plaster or plasterboard first with a plaster primer or with a coat of emulsion paint thinned with a little water. If the walls are papered, stick down any loose seams and patch any tears before starting painting (see page 81).

What to do

The secret of success when painting walls and ceilings is to divide the area up into bands of a manageable width – about 1m (3ft or so) is ideal. If the surface has been papered and you can still see the seam lines, use these instead as natural dividers. Start applying paint in a corner of the room, completing one band before moving along to the next and blending the edges of the areas carefully as you work.

Use a 75mm or 100mm (3 or 4in) brush, a 180mm or 230mm (7 or 9in) roller or a large wall pad to apply the paint. With a roller you will have to brush a band of paint around wall and ceiling perimeters first, since the roller will not reach right into the corners.

Make sure you are working in good light so you can check that you are applying the paint evenly and are not missing any areas. When painting ceilings, it is best to start by the window and work across the room so light from the window is reflected and shows up any missed.

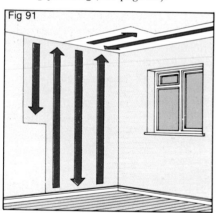

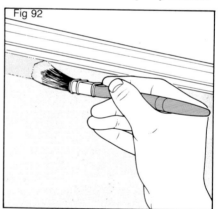

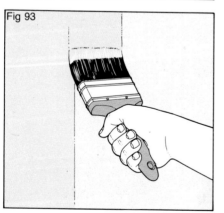

Fig 91   When you are painting walls and ceilings, always start work near the window so the light will help you see where you have painted. Apply the paint in overlapping bands.

Fig 92   Start by using a small brush to paint into angles where a larger brush or a paint roller will not reach.

Fig 93   Use a 75mm (3in) or 100mm (4in) wide brush to apply the paint, brushing first one way and then at right angles to get even coverage.

Fig 94   With a roller, work in broad overlapping bands. Do not overstretch and risk a fall when working on steps.

Painting Doors

Painting or varnishing a door is a perfect DIY job if you have a couple of hours to spare, and can transform a dowdy, chipped and finger-marked old feature into a gleaming new entrance to any room.

As with painting walls and ceilings, the secret of success lies in the preparation. Since doorways have to put up with a lot of through traffic, the door and its frame will at the very least be covered in greasy fingermarks, and the finish may well be scratched or chipped too. The first step therefore is to put a dust sheet down beneath it, and to remove knobs and other furniture so you can wash the paintwork down with detergent or sugar soap. Then fill any blemishes with filler or by touching them in with a little quick-drying primer-undercoat (painted doors only), and rub the surface with fine abrasive paper to provide a key for the new finish.

Wedge the door open while you work and push a timber peg into the spindle hole on each side so you will be able to move the door easily while you decorate it without touching wet paint or varnish.

What to do

If you are painting a panelled door, start with the panels first. Begin with one of the top panels and brush paint lightly into the mouldings, taking care not to create runs at edges or a paint build-up in corners. Then paint the centre of each panel before moving on to the next. When all the panels have been completed, paint the muntins (the vertical dividers between the panels) and the horizontal rails, finishing off with the stiles that run the full length of the door at each side.

With flush doors, start painting at the top and sub-divide the door surface up into six or eight imaginary squares. Paint one, then its neighbour, blending them together carefully so the overlap is not visible.

With glazed doors, use masking tape to keep paint off the glass and paint the glazing beads first, then the rest of the door. Remove the tape when the paint is just touch-dry.

Complete the door by painting the other side and the two long edges.

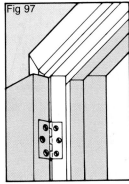

Fig 97 (*above*) Where you are using different colours in adjoining rooms, paint the face of the door stop bead to match the colour on the closing face of the door.

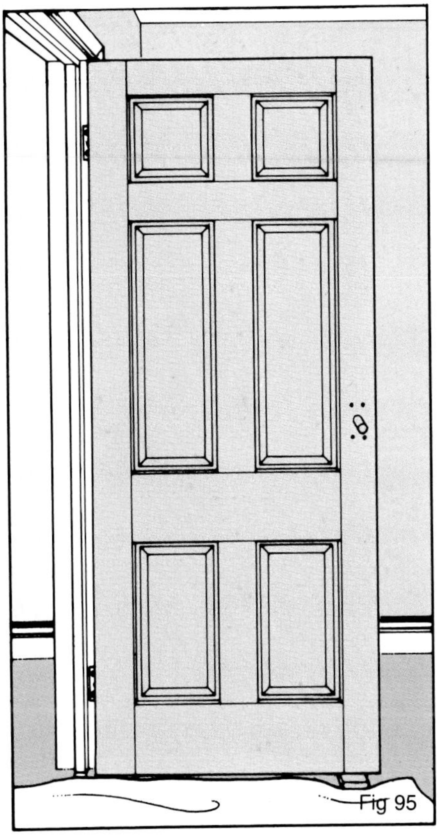

Fig 95 When painting a door, open it and put down a dust sheet underneath it. Then remove all door furniture and wedge the door from both sides.

On a panelled door paint the mouldings first, then the panels. Do the horizontal rails next, and finish off with the vertical stiles.

Fig 96 On a flush door, divide the surface up into six or eight imaginary squares and paint each one in turn before doing the adjoining square.

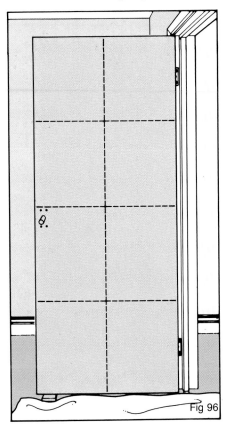

Fig 95

Fig 96

Painting Windows

Windows are generally much more fiddly and time-consuming to paint, especially if they have small panes of glass and lots of glazing beads. Not only are many of the surfaces difficult to reach comfortably unless you are ambidextrous; you also have to take care to keep paint off the glass as far as possible while you work.

It is best to plan the repainting of a window as a two-stage job, with the interior and exterior surfaces being tackled as two related but separate jobs (see pages 68–9 for details of how to paint outdoor woodwork).

As with all painting jobs, the key to success is thorough preparation, and this is particularly important with windows because over-zealous painting can cause them to jam shut. Start by washing down the paint surfaces, using fungicide to kill any black mould that has begun to grow on the internal bedding putty as a result of condensation. Then sand down the paintwork lightly to provide a key for the new paint film. If opening casements are already a tight fit, plane the binding edges.

What to do

Sash windows are the most difficult to paint because part of the sash sides are hidden at each side of the frame. If you need to replace the sash cords, it is a good opportunity to remove the sashes from their frames and paint them on your workbench, but you are more likely to have to paint them *in situ*. Start by reversing the sashes and paint as much as you can of the outer sash plus the lower rail and underside of the inner sash. Also paint the lower part of the frame within which the inner sash slides.

Next return the sashes to their normal positions so you can paint the rest of the outer sash, the inner sash and the upper part of the frame in which the inner sash slides. Finally, paint the frame surround. Tackle painting the part of the frame in which the outer sash slides from outside.

Casement windows are much simpler. Paint any glazing bars and the rebates first, then do the casement rails and stiles and finish by painting the frame itself.

What you need:
- screwdriver
- paint brush or pad
- masking tape

TIP
Try to pick a still day when painting windows, to minimize the risk of wind-blown dust marring the new paint finish. When painting casement windows, place small wood blocks in the bottom of the rebates to prevent them from closing on wet paint.

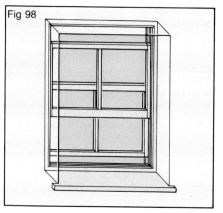

Fig 98

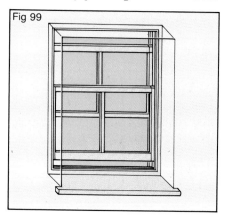

Fig 99

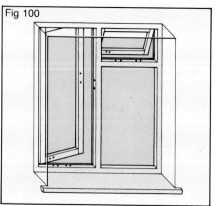

Fig 100

Fig 101

Fig 98 To paint a sash window, first push the inner sash up and pull the inner sash down. Paint the inner sash and the lower part of the outer sash, plus the lower part of the groove in which the inner sash slides.

Fig 99 When the paint is touch-dry, reverse the sashes so you can paint the upper part of the outer sash and the upper part of the groove in which the inner sash slides. Then paint the frame and sill.

Fig 100 To paint a casement window, remove the window furniture. Then paint the opening casement and top light first, followed by their rebates. Finish off by painting the rest of the frame and the sill.

Fig 101 Unless you have a very steady hand, use masking tape to get a neat paint line that extends onto the glass by about 3mm (⅛in). Remove the tape when the paint is touch-dry.

Painting Mouldings and Radiators

The interiors of most homes are decorated with a variety of timber mouldings – door architraves, picture or dado rails, skirting boards and so on. These are usually painted to match other interior woodwork, although they may as an alternative be stained and varnished (*see* page 42). Radiators and their pipework are also painted to decorate and protect them. Prepare the surfaces by washing them down and then keying the old paint with fine abrasive.

What to do

Use a narrow brush to paint mouldings, especially if they have a complex cross section with grooves in which excess paint could gather. Take care not to get paint on adjoining wall surfaces (although if they are bare and will be papered, taking the paint a little way onto the wall will help disguise the join when the paper is hung). Use a paint shield to keep paint off the floor when painting skirting boards.

Always turn radiators off and allow them to cool down before you paint them.

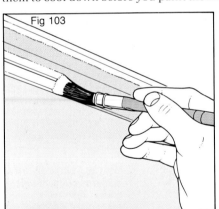

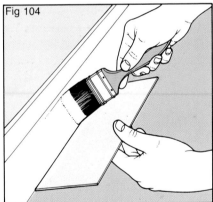

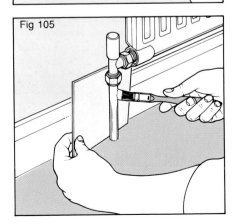

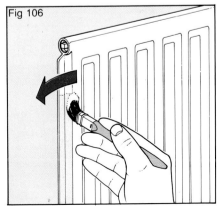

Fig 102 (*above*) You can paint door architrave mouldings to match the colour used on the door.

Fig 103 Use a small brush to paint features such as cornices, picture and dado rails.

Fig 104 Unless you can lift floorcoverings easily, use a paint shield to keep paint off the floor surface when painting skirting boards.

Fig 105 Paint radiator pipework and other pipes to match the colour of woodwork or walls behind them so they blend in unobtrusively.

Fig 106 Paint radiators to match walls or woodwork. Avoid a paint build-up along seams and edges by brushing towards the edge, not across it.

Staining and Varnishing Wood

Many people prefer the natural look of wood as an alternative to a paint finish, often enhancing the grain pattern by using wood stains and then protecting the surface with varnish. Apart from its attractive appearance, wood decorated in this way also shows everyday wear and tear less than a painted surface; dirty marks are less obvious, and chips and scratches are not nearly as noticeable.

If you are working with new wood, simply ensure that the surface is smooth and free from greasy finger-marks. Wash down and key existing stained and varnished wood before giving it a facelift with a fresh coat of varnish. If you want to stain and varnish wood that currently has a paint finish, you must strip this off completely first using either a chemical paint stripper or a hot air gun. Take care not to char the wood if you use a hot air gun, and ensure good ventilation when working indoors with chemical strippers. As an alternative, you can send removable things like doors to a professional firm to be stripped by dipping in caustic soda.

What to do

Start by deciding what depth and colour of stain you want to apply. For a relatively weak depth of colour, the quickest method of decorating the wood is to use a coloured varnish; this is available in a range of wood shades as well as some bright primary colours. Simply apply two coats to the wood surface, thinning the first coat with a little white spirit.

For deeper staining it is better to use separate stain and varnish applications. Test the stain first on an unobtrusive part of the surface you are decorating, and dilute it if necessary to get a weaker colour or mix it with other stains to get the precise shade you want. Then apply the stain with a cloth, working along the grain in touching but not overlapping bands. Apply a second coat when the first is dry for a deeper colour. When the stain is dry, sand the surface very lightly to remove any raised wood fibres, dust it and apply two coats of varnish to seal in the stain and protect the surface.

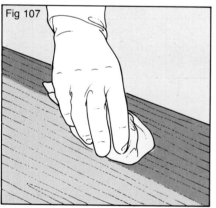

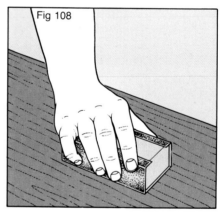

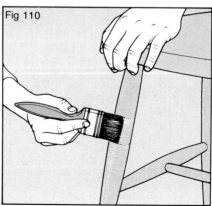

Fig 107 Sand wood to be stained until it feels smooth to your fingers. Then apply the stain with a clean cloth pad, wiping it on in adjacent but not overlapping bands. Always work along the grain.

Fig 108 When you have achieved the right depth of colour, sand the surface very lightly with fine abrasive paper to remove any raised wood fibres, ready for varnishing.

Fig 109 Apply varnish as you would paint, brushing on along the grain initially and then across it to get even coverage. Finish off with very light brush strokes along the grain.

Fig 110 On curved surfaces, take care to avoid runs by brushing round the curvature first, then finishing off along the grain as for flat surfaces.

Using Textured Finishes

Textured finishes are an attractive alternative to relief wallcoverings if you want a three-dimensional surface to your walls and ceilings. They are also an excellent cover-up for less-than-perfect plasterwork on which you do not want to spend a lot of preparation time before painting or paperhanging in the usual way.

There are two main types of textured finish available. The first comes in powder form; you simply add water to make up a creamy mix which you apply to the surface you are decorating, ready for texturing. Artex is the most widely available brand; indeed, the name has become synonymous with textured finishes in the same way as Formica is plastic laminate for kitchen worktops. It is now also available in ready-mixed form.

The second finish is better known as textured emulsion paint, and gives a less pronounced relief finish to the surface. It is ready to apply straight from the tub.

Most of these finishes dry white or off-white, and can be painted using emulsion if you want a coloured finish.

What to do

You can apply textured finishes to any wall or ceiling surface so long as it is properly prepared. That means washing down existing painted surfaces with sugar soap or strong detergent, removing any flaking material and filling large cracks. You must remove wallcoverings completely.

With powder types, mix the contents of a 5kg (11lb) bag with 2¼ litres (4 pints) of water, leave to stand for 10 minutes and then add a further ½ litre (1 pint) of water. Stir thoroughly. Ready-mixed types can be applied direct from the tub.

Apply powder and thick ready-mixed types with a wide paintbrush; use a roller if you prefer with textured emulsion paints. Cover an area of about 2sq m (22sq ft) at a time, then texture the freshly-applied coating with whatever tools you have decided to use – a sponge, a stippling brush or a proprietary texture roller. At wall edges and round obstacles, use a narrower brush to form an untextured band that will 'frame' the textured area neatly.

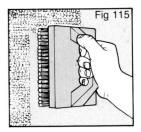
Fig 115

Fig 115 (*above*) Texture the finish by stippling it, creating swirls with a brush or comb, or by running a texturing roller over it.

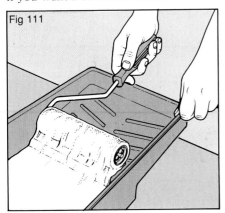
Fig 111

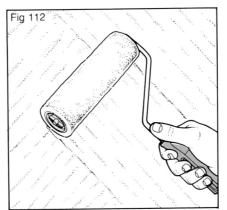
Fig 112

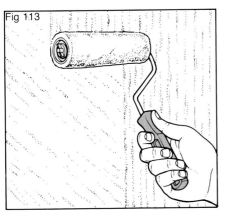
Fig 113

Fig 114

Fig 111 Pour textured finish into a roller tray and load your roller generously.

Fig 112 Apply the finish with overlapping diagonal strokes.

Fig 113 Finish off with vertical strokes.

Fig 114 Use a brush to smooth off the texture at ceiling edges and round obstacles.

Creating Special Paint Effects

Painted walls and woodwork do not have to be just one colour; there are lots of special paint effects you can use to liven up their appearance. Some are purely decorative; others actually imitate the look of other materials. They are all very inexpensive to create, and with a little patience and practice you can achieve quite stunning results.

These decorative effects fall into two broad categories – broken colour and imitation. In the first category, various techniques are used to apply a second colour over a different-coloured basecoat so that the latter still shows through, creating a pleasing two-colour effect. In the second category, paint is used to give the surface the appearance of another material; expensive wood veneers, marble and tortoiseshell are among the most popular effects you can create.

Whichever one you are trying to achieve, careful preparation of the surface of the wall or woodwork you are planning to decorate is essential if you are to get good results.

What to do

If the surface is already painted and the finish is sound, wash it down, attend to any surface blemishes and then apply a coat of the base colour you have chosen. Your next step is to decide which effect you want. These are the most popular.

Sponging involves using a piece of sponge to dab irregular patches of colour over a contrasting basecoat.

Stippling with a special stippling brush gives a plain finish an attractive mottled effect, and is often used to obliterate brush marks before applying another effect.

Ragging involves using pads or rolls of screwed-up cotton rag or other fabric to apply a random second colour to the surface. Using a pad gives a finish similar to sponging, while rag-rolling creates an effect resembling crushed silk.

Bag graining gives a rather finer textured finish than rag-rolling – more like crushed velvet – and is created by pressing a polythene bag filled with crumpled rags onto the wet paint surface.

What you need:
- base colours
- special effect colours
- paint brush, roller or pad
- paint kettle, roller tray or pad loading tray
- sponge
- rags
- graining brush
- stencils
- stencilling brush
- masking tape

CHECK
- that the base colour is completely dry before starting to apply the special effect.

TIP
Use emulsion paint test pots to provide small amounts of paint for special effects.

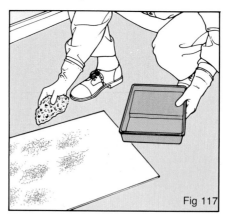

Fig 116

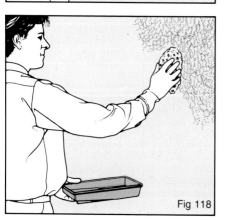

Fig 118

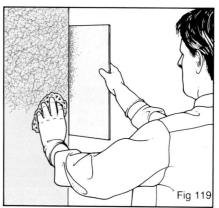

Fig 119

Fig 116   Start by applying your base colour evenly to the surface being decorated, using a roller or brush.

Fig 117   Test the effect you want to achieve on an offcut of board or other surface. Here a sponge is being used to create a sponged effect.

Fig 118   Move to the wall, dip the sponge in the paint and apply light pressure to create overlapping splodges of colour on the surface.

Fig 119   Use a mask to keep paint off adjoining surfaces if these are not being decorated in the same way.

Creating Special Paint Effects

Dragging involves drawing a dry brush over the wet paint surface to produce parallel lines of colour with the base coat colour showing through the top coat.

Graining is a staining process used to make a bland, uninteresting wood resemble something more exotic by copying its colours and figuring.

Marbling involves blending a mixture of wet colours to create the effect of coloured natural stone.

Tortoise-shelling, as its name implies, is another imitative effect created by blending wet colours on a suitable base coat – again best used in small doses.

Stencilling is different to the other techniques, and involves applying paint through a stencil to create a motif or design on top of the base coat.

It is a good idea to experiment on some scrap material before starting work on the actual surface you are decorating. This gives you a chance to assess how the finished product will look, and perhaps to modify the depth of colour or the strength of the applied effect.

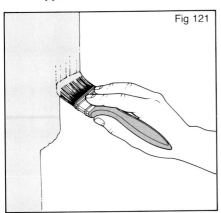

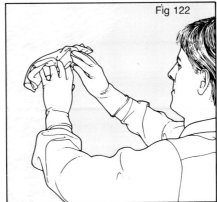

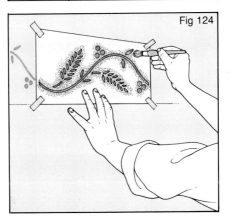

Fig 120 (*above*) Sponging and other paint effects create a delicacy of colour that no other technique can match.

Fig 121 For rag-rolling, brush on the base colour generously.

Fig 122 Then use the rolled-up rag with a rocking motion to 'lift' paint from the surface.

Fig 123 For graining, apply the stain to the surface and then draw a dry brush over it along the grain direction.

Fig 124 For stencilling, tape the stencil to the wall and dab paint through it with a special stiff-bristled stencilling brush.

Papering a Room

Hanging new wallcoverings all round a room is a major decorating project that needs careful planning if it is to proceed smoothly. Rather like painting walls, the job involves endless repetition of one basic task – hanging a length of wallpaper – but within any room you are likely to encounter a number of obstacles and each one will need tackling in a different way if you are to get good results.

The first thing to do when planning to paper a room is to clear the room of as much furniture as possible. If it must remain in the room, group it together in the centre and cover it with dust sheets. Then take down all pictures and other wall-mounted items such as shelves, curtain tracks and wall lights. Where items will have to be replaced in the same position, insert match sticks into the wallplugs so they will pierce the new wallpaper as it is hung and make it easy to identify the screw positions. Turn the power to wall lights off first, and wrap PVC insulating tape round the exposed cables once you have disconnected and removed the lights.

What to do

With the room clear you can start planning exactly how to tackle the job. If your room has a chimney breast or some other prominent feature such as a dormer window and you are hanging a paper with a bold design motif, it is best to centre the first length on the feature concerned. Otherwise, the best place to start papering is near a corner of the room – ideally on the longest uninterrupted wall.

When you have chosen your starting point, use a roll of wallpaper as a gauge and mark the walls round the room with the approximate positions of the joins. This will enable you to see whether any will fall in awkward places – on the external corners of chimney breasts or window reveals, for example – and will allow you to alter your starting point accordingly.

You are now ready to start hanging the new wallcovering in earnest. Plumb a line on the wall at your chosen starting point and paste and hang your first length. Then carry on hanging subsequent lengths on

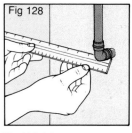

Fig 128 (*above*) Where a pipe passes through a wall, measure its distance from the edge of the last length and make a cut in the edge of the next length.

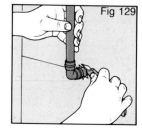

Fig 129 (*above*) Hang the length round the pipe, trimming it to a precise fit.

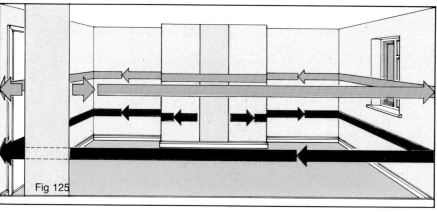

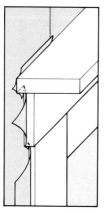

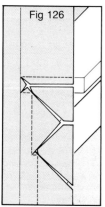

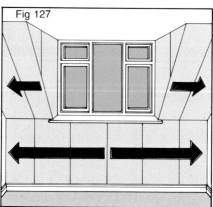

Fig 125 Start hanging at the centre of a chimney breast if the paper has a dominant pattern. Otherwise start next to the room door.

Fig 126 Make release cuts to allow the paper to be fitted and trimmed round obstacles such as fireplaces.

Fig 127 Work outwards from the centre of a dormer window so lengths are centred on the window recess.

the first wall, dealing with small obstacles such as light switches and power points by making diagonal cuts over their positions and trimming the tongues (*see* page 25). To fit the tongues neatly behind the accessory faceplate, turn off the power and loosen the fixing screws. Tuck the paper in and re-tighten the screws.

At radiators, make cuts up from the bottom of the length in line with the positions of the radiator brackets and tuck the paper down behind the radiator with a slim long-handled paint roller.

At fireplaces, let one edge of the length of paper that will overlap it touch the edge of the mantel shelf, and make a release cut into it so you can brush the upper part of the length onto the wall above it. Then make further cuts so you can trim the lower part of the length to fit.

Arches are particularly difficult to cope with. Paper the face wall(s) and the back wall of an arched recess first, making lots of small release cuts so you can turn the paper onto the arch sides. Then cut and hang separate strips on the arch itself.

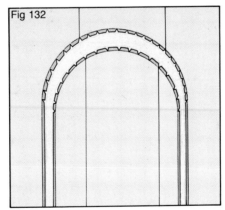

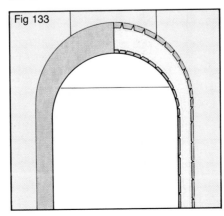

Fig 130 (*above*) Stick to papers with small random patterns on complex surfaces such as this sloping attic ceiling.

Fig 131 Paper the face walls flanking a through arch first, turning about 25mm (1in) of paper onto the arch surface after making small release cuts in the edges. Then cut a strip of paper long enough to cover the arch surface and brush it into place, working from the bottom upwards.

Fig 132 Paper the face and back walls of an arched recess first, then paper the arch itself as described.

Fig 133 With papers having a strongly directional pattern rather than a random one, paper the arch with two separate strips running from the head of the arch down to the floor at each side.

Hanging Speciality Wallcoverings

Most of your paper-hanging will involve using either printed papers of one type or another or else a relief wallpaper such as woodchip or Anaglypta. However, there are also several speciality wallcoverings which you may want to hang on small areas for their decorative effect (most are too expensive to use for a whole room). These include hessian, flocks, grasscloth, silks and other printed fabrics, and a range of woolstrand wallcoverings. All have a paper backing to make them easier to hang, although hessian is also available un-backed. Most are sold by the metre.

Some of them are hung like conventional wallcoverings, with the paste being applied to the paper; others are hung by pasting the wall with a heavy-duty ready-mixed tub paste and then unrolling the wallcovering onto it. A unique printed wallcovering called Novamura, which is made from foamed polyethylene with no paper backing, is also hung in this way. Check which hanging method the wall-covering manufacturer recommends when you are choosing these products.

What to do

If the wallcovering is hung by pasting the backing paper, you must take great care to keep paste off the front of the material as you apply it or staining may result. Keep your pasting table scrupulously clean and fold lengths with great care. If any paste does get onto the face of the length, wipe it off immediately with a damp sponge. Hang the lengths as for any other wall-covering, using a paper-hanging brush or a paint roller to smooth them into place.

If the recommendation is to paste the wall, mark the width to be coated and apply the paste with a broad brush or a paint roller. Then roll the length loosely onto a length of broomstick from the bottom to the top, and get a helper to support the roll while you position the top edge on the wall and smooth the length downwards into position.

Novamura is light enough not to need supporting in this way; you can simply hold the rolled-up length in your other hand as you smooth it onto the wall.

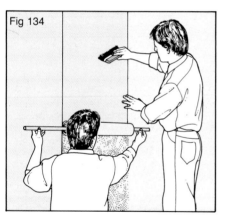

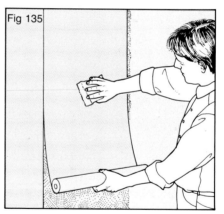

Fig 134   Roll lengths of fabric and other speciality wallcoverings round a broomstick, and get a helper to hold it while you smooth the length onto the wall.

Fig 135   With Novamura, paste the wall first and then hang the material straight from the roll. Smooth it in place with a brush or sponge.

Fig 136   If you have to trim the edges of fabric wallcoverings, overlap them with a strip of lining paper in between. Then use a sharp knife and a straightedge to cut through all three layers, peel off the waste and brush the seam back into place.

Fig 137   Use a roller to press fabric and other speciality wallcoverings into place.

Papering Ceilings

There are two main reasons why you might want to use wallcoverings to decorate your ceilings. The first is purely aesthetic – because it may look better with some pattern or texture as an alternative to the use of plain flat colour. The second is more mundanely practical – a means of covering up a less than perfect ceiling surface.

There is nothing to stop you using any wallcovering material on your ceilings, although in practice few people use patterned types which would need stripping and replacing at regular intervals, preferring instead to put up plain relief papers which are then painted and repainted as the years go by. There is a good reason for this: papering a ceiling can appear tricky enough, but stripping old wallpaper off one is even more awkward.

In fact, once you have got used to the concept of hanging wallpaper 'upside-down' you will find that papering a ceiling is actually easier than papering any but the plainest, flattest wall because the surface is free of the awkward obstructions which get in the way of most wallpapering.

What to do

The key to success when papering a ceiling is to set up sensible access equipment; you cannot work safely stepping from dining chair to orange box and back again. Hire a pair of decorators' trestles and some scaffold boards or lightweight staging from a local plant hire firm so you can create a room-wide platform at a comfortable height. Trestles can also be used as stepladders when you want to reach up and trim the ends of individual lengths at each side of the ceiling. It is also a good idea to have a helper who can support the folded lengths as you hang them.

Use a string line pinned across the room just less than the roll width away from one wall to mark a line against which the first length will be hung. Position one end in the wall/ceiling angle, aligned with the line, and brush it into place just like hanging wallpaper. Trim the ends and the long edge, then hang subsequent lengths. Pierce the paper at light positions and trim it neatly to fit round the rose.

What you need:
- stepladders and scaffold boards or
- trestles and lightweight staging
- paper-hanging tools
- a helper

CHECK
- that you turn the power off at the mains before undoing ceiling rose covers to tuck paper behind them.

TIP
Remove pendant light fittings before starting to paper a ceiling.

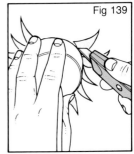

Fig 139 (*above*) Pierce the length at light positions, make release cuts all round and then trim the paper neatly.

Fig 138

Fig 138 (*left*) Papering ceilings is really a two-person job. Set up a working platform running the full width of the room, and chalk a string line across the ceiling just less than the width of the paper from the side wall. Brush the first length into place along the string line, while your helper supports the rest of the length. Then move the platform and hang the next length.

Papering Stairwells

Stairwells pose two main problems as far as decorating is concerned; the need for suitable access equipment to enable you to reach the top of walls that are effectively two storeys high (which applies whether you are painting or paper-hanging and the problems of handling and hanging extra-long lengths of wallcovering material. The longest drop in a stairwell may be as much as 5m (16ft) or thereabouts – the equivalent of half a roll in length. Not only is this much wet pasted paper difficult to handle, even with a helper; there is also the problem of stretch as the length is hung, posing problems of pattern matching unless care is taken.

For this reason it is best to choose a wallcovering that has a 'free' pattern match (or none at all) and is relatively strong when wet. The best choice is a heavy-duty vinyl wallcovering, which will also withstand wear and tear well, but a heavy relief wallcovering such as Supaglypta would also be a good choice. Avoid thin lightweight printed papers wherever possible.

What to do

Start by assessing how best to provide the safe access you need. You can arrange a combination of sections of extension ladder and stepladders to support scaffold boards or lightweight staging at the required height within the stairwell (see below), or else use the components of a slot-together platform tower to build a working platform within the stairwell (see page 36 for details of this and for an access arrangement for L-shaped flights). Ladders, steps and scaffold boards generally take up less space than a tower, making it easier to move about on the staircase.

Hang the longest drop first, with your helper supporting the folded paper while you brush it into place against a plumbed line. Measure the length of each piece against the edge of the last piece hung to ensure that it will be cut long enough, and trim the bottom of each length to match the slope of the staircase string. Where a handrail meets a papered wall, make small release cuts and trim the paper to fit.

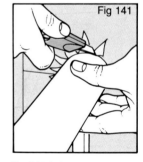

Fig 141 (*above*) Where a handrail runs into a wall, make release cuts to fit the paper round the rail, and trim the paper to a neat fit.

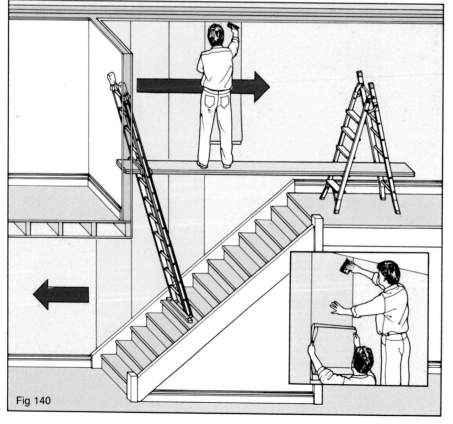

Fig 140

Fig 140 (*left*) When papering a stairwell, first set up a suitable access platform so you can reach all the walls. Then hang the longest drop first, and work along the side wall towards the landing. Get a helper to support the lower part of each length while you position and hang the upper part, to avoid unnecessary stretching.

Putting up Friezes and Borders

Friezes and borders are decorative features with a long pedigree. They are basically narrow strips of printed paper or vinyl, often in colours and designs that complement wallcoverings and fabrics from the same manufacturer. Friezes are used to apply a band of colour round a room, usually at roughly picture-rail height or above dados, while borders are used to frame features of the room – a door opening or an archway, for example – or to create framed panels on a wall or ceiling surface. They come in a range of widths.

Some friezes and borders are intended to be pasted just like wallpaper, while others are self-adhesive. The former are ideal for use on walls that have been painted or decorated with a plain printed wallpaper, but will not stick to a washable or vinyl wallcovering unless special overlap adhesive is used instead of ordinary paste; here a self-adhesive type is a better bet.

It is a good idea to experiment with the positioning of friezes and borders before sticking them up permanently, using masking tape to hold them in place.

What to do

Once you have decided on the precise positioning of your frieze or border, draw light pencil guidelines on the wall or ceiling surface as a guide to help you position them accurately. For friezes, use a spirit level to ensure that the guideline is truly horizontal; for borders, use a plumbline and square as well to ensure that sections meet at right angles.

With types that need pasting, apply the paste as for ordinary wallcoverings, taking care not to get paste on the face if it is a plain printed type. Then fold the length up concertina-fashion, carry it to the wall, offer up one end to the guideline and brush it into position. If you have to butt-join lengths, overlap one on the other with the pattern aligned and cut through both with a sharp knife. Use the same technique to form perfectly mitred corners.

With self-adhesive types, peel off some of the backing paper and position one end, then peel and stick the rest of the length in place bit by bit.

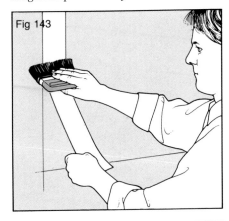

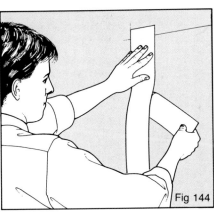

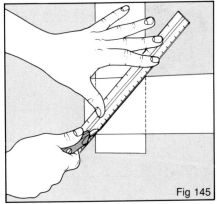

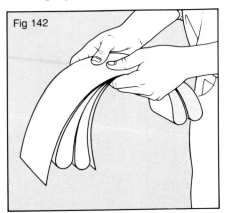

Fig 142 Paste and fold friezes and borders as for full-sized lengths of wallcovering, and carry the folded length to the wall.

Fig 143 Draw guidelines on the wall and then line up the length and brush it into place.

Fig 144 Use guidelines with self-adhesive types too. Peel off some of the backing paper and position one end of the length, then peel and stick the rest.

Fig 145 To form neatly-mitred corners with borders, overlap the adjacent lengths and cut through both with a sharp knife and a straightedge. Then peel off and discard the waste and roll the seam.

Putting Up Coving

Coving or cornice – the two terms seem to be used interchangeably nowadays – is a moulding that is fixed into the angle between walls and ceilings for decorative effect. The moulding may be a plain quadrant in cross-section with a smooth surface along its length, or may be a highly elaborate affair with a three-dimensional pattern.

The cheapest coving is made from polystyrene, the white granular plastic widely used in packaging. More expensive is the plain plasterboard coving often used by property developers in new houses; this has a plaster core encased in stout paper, and is available only with a plain quadrant cross-section. Most expensive are the various moulded types, made either from fibrous plaster (the traditional material) or from cellular plastics. The latter are excellent imitations of fibrous plaster without the weight, and are much easier to install as a result.

Apart from its decorative effect, coving can also help to disguise the cracks that often open up between walls and ceilings.

What to do

Start by measuring the length of each wall in the room. Then choose the type of coving you want, and find out in what lengths it is made so you can work out how many will be needed for each wall. You must allow for cutting mitres at internal and external corners, so it is better to over-estimate slightly.

Start by cutting a mitre on one end of the first length to be installed. Make up a mitre box from scrap timber, wide enough to hold the coving with the edge that will go against the ceiling in the bottom of the box, and make sure you are making the correct cut for the mitre position (see Figs 150 and 151). Apply the coving adhesive and stick the length in place. Then mitre and fit the next length at the other end of this wall, before butt-jointing intermediate sections into place between the two. Repeat this sequence on the other walls, cutting mitres correctly as required to make up internal and external corners (see Fig 151 again).

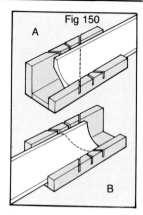

Fig 150 (*above*) Make these mitre cuts (A and B) for external corners.

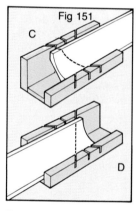

Fig 151 (*above*) Make these cuts (C and D) for internal corners.

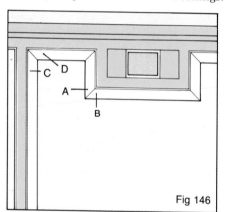

Fig 146

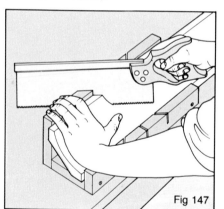

Fig 147

Fig 148

Fig 149

Fig 146 Coving has mitred corners, with different cuts for the left and right hand part at internal and external corners (*see* Figs 150-1).

Fig 147 Make a mitre box to hold the coving with its ceiling edge on the base of the box.

Fig 148 Cut the mitre and fix the first length in place. Then fix the mitred piece at the other end of the wall.

Fig 149 Fill in between these two lengths with square-cut sections.

Tiling a Room

The rooms where you might decide to have wall-to-wall tiling are your kitchen, your bathroom, a separate WC or a shower room. In each case the reason is the durability and water-resistance of the surface – both major advantages in rooms where there is a lot of water vapour and you want walls that are easy to keep clean. However, tiling on this scale does have its disadvantages too. For a start it is likely to prove very expensive. Tiles are also the most difficult wallcovering of all to change if you tire of the colour or design, and can make condensation problems worse because the surface is cold to the touch, especially when the tiles are fixed to an external wall. You should weigh all these points up carefully before going ahead.

Assuming that you do, you have the same prospect as painting and papering a room; carrying out the same basic operation over and over again to fix the hundreds of tiles in place. Success and the avoidance of problems depends entirely on the care and attention you give to setting out the tiling arrangement (see page 27).

What to do

When you have completed the setting-out to your satisfaction, your next step is to remove any wall-mounted fittings – shelves, wall lights, mirrors, curtain rails and toilet-roll holders in a bathroom, for example. Then mark up your starting points on each wall, and pin guide battens in place to support the lowest row of whole tiles all round the room, and also the rows of whole tiles over window and door openings. You can then start tiling.

Begin with the most difficult wall – probably the one containing the window, if the room has one. Fix all the whole tiles first, then add cut pieces as required. Leave the horizontal battens in place for 24 hours, then remove them and fit the cut pieces at skirting-board level. It is a good idea to grout each wall as you complete it, before moving on to tile the next wall, as a way of breaking the monotony of the job.

When all the tiling and grouting is complete, drill fixing holes where required and replace the wall-mounted fittings.

What you need:
- tiles
- tile adhesive
- grout
- tiling equipment
- tile battens
- hammer and masonry nails

(*See also* pages 26–30)

Fig 152 The secret of success when tiling a whole room lies in the setting out (*see* page 27). If you have done this carefully, centring the tile layout on each wall to take account of obstacles such as window recesses, the actual tiling will be no more difficult than tackling a small splashback.

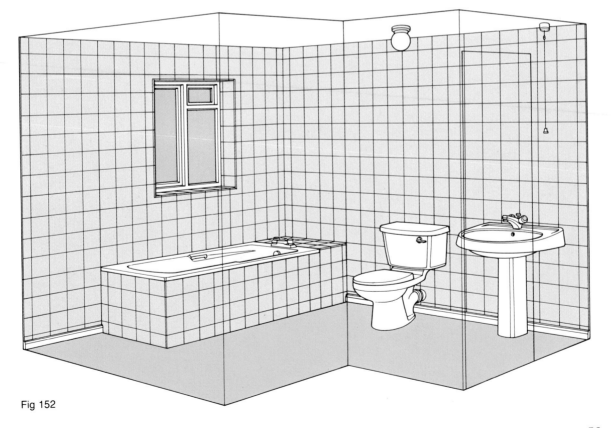

Fig 152

Cladding Walls

Wooden panelling of one sort or another has been a popular way of decorating interior walls for centuries. It is good-looking, hard-wearing and warm to the touch, and can be crafted and finished in several different ways. One of the most popular effects is the use of tongue-and-groove boards. Softwood, often described as 'knotty pine', is the obvious choice, but other more exotic woods can be used instead if you can find supplies.

Apart from its looks, cladding has other advantages. For a start, it is the perfect cover-up for walls with defective (or missing) plaster. It feels warm to the touch, so helps to cut down condensation, and if insulation is fitted behind it the result is a much warmer room – a particular boon in properties with solid walls which are difficult to insulate. Lastly, it can help to reduce noise transmission between rooms. The only drawback is that the room is made slightly smaller, and some repositioning of fittings such as radiators, wall lights, switches and power points may be necessary.

What to do

Start fixing battens at the top and sides of the wall to be clad, and at floor level if you have removed the skirting. Then add intermediate battens at about 600mm (2ft) intervals across the wall, and fix short battens round switch or socket mounting boxes to support the cladding.

Cut the first board to length and offer it up to one edge of the area to be clad with the grooved edge in the corner. Use a spirit level to ensure that it is vertical, then scribe the profile of the side wall and its skirting board onto its face. Use a jigsaw to cut along the marked line, then nail it to the battens with panel pins driven at an angle through the exposed tongue. Add another pin driven into each batten through the face of the board.

Fix the second board by sliding its grooved edge over the tongue of the first board. Then drive pins through its tongue as before. Repeat this process to fix all the other full-length boards to the battens. Leave the last length, which will have to

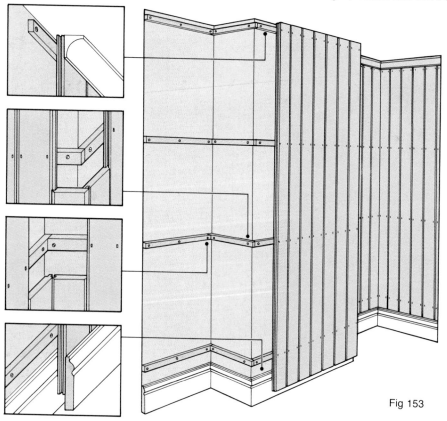

Fig 153

Fig 153 Tongue-and-groove timber cladding is secured to horizontal wall battens at floor and ceiling level and at roughly 750mm (2ft 6in) intervals in between. Cut the boards to leave a narrow air gap at the ceiling and floor; these are covered by lengths of scotia beading and a new skirting board. Form butt joints at internal and external corners, with the exposed board edge planed smooth at external corners for a neat finish.

Cladding Walls

be scribed to fit, until later. To fix cladding round a light switch or socket outlet, make small cut-outs in the adjacent boards before fitting them.

At internal corners, the last length must be scribed and cut down to width. Pin or hold it on top of the last whole board fitted, and use an offcut of cladding to scribe the wall profile back onto the board. Cut along the scribed line with a jig saw, offer the board up into position and fix it to the battens with pins driven through the board face.

However carefully you work, the cut ends of the boards will always look a little ragged. Neaten them off by adding slim quadrant beading at ceiling and wall edges, and replace the skirting board at floor level. With all the boards and trims in place, sand the wall surface down lightly and wipe the board surfaces down with a clean, lint-free cloth dampened with white spirit to remove dust, ready for the final finish to be applied. You can varnish the boards as they are, apply stain first or even use paint if you prefer.

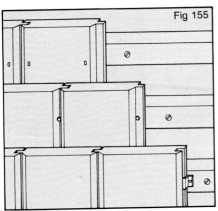

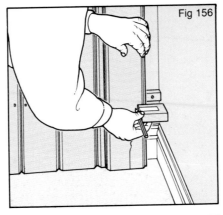

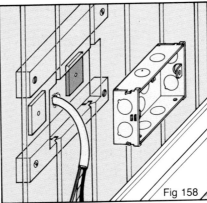

Fig 154 (*above*) Timber cladding gives any room a warm, natural appearance.

Fig 155 You can fix the cladding to the wall battens in one of three ways – by nailing through the board face, by secret nailing through the tongues or by using proprietary fixing clips.

Fig 156 At internal corners, scribe the edge of the last board so it matches the profile of the side wall.

Fig 157 At window reveals, finish the cladding neatly with a corner batten.

Fig 158 Reposition flush wiring accessories so their faceplates finish flush with the cladding.

Laying Carpets

Foam-backed carpets need no underlay and can be fixed in place with heavy-duty double-sided adhesive tape, so are relatively easy for the inexperienced to lay in a room without too many awkward obstructions. Putting one down in, say, a bedroom will be valuable practice before moving on to laying hessian-backed carpet, which must be stretched across the room and held in place with toothed gripper strips all round the room's perimeter. This tension is necessary to ensure that the pile is upright, improving the carpet's durability. Hessian-backed carpets must always be laid over a foam underlay, which is cut to fit within the gripper strips and should be stapled to timber floors or stuck to concrete ones with double-sided tape to stop it moving beneath the carpet.

Carpets are sold by the metre, almost exclusively in 4m (13ft) widths, so you will need seams only in large rooms. Whichever type is laid, doorways are finished off with special threshold strips which hold the carpet edge securely and prevent any risk of tripping.

What to do

If you are laying a **foam-backed carpet**, cover the floor first of all with special glass fibre underlay sheeting or stout brown paper. This stops dust working its way into the back of the carpet, and also helps to prevent the foam sticking to the floor in heavy traffic areas. Lay it to within about 50mm (2in) of the skirting board, and tape it down. Then run double-sided adhesive tape round the room between the skirting board and the underlay, leaving the release paper on.

Unroll the carpet parallel to the longest wall in the room, allowing the ends and the other long side to lap up the skirting board. Secure the long edge with the double-sided tape, then make release cuts at all the internal and external corners to allow the carpet to lie flat.

Tread the carpet into place by shuffling your feet across to the opposite long wall, and then trim off the excess using a sharp handyman's knife held at an angle of 45° to the floor and pressed into the angle

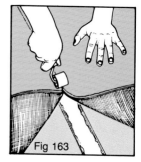

Fig 163 (*above*) Use a seam roller to bond seams to the adhesive tape.

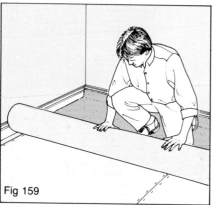

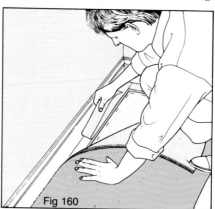

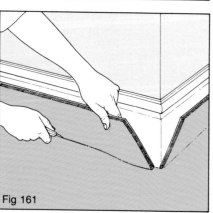

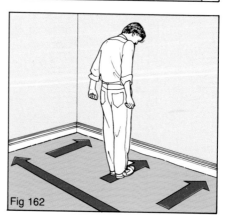

Fig 159 To lay a foam-backed carpet, put down underlay and stick double-sided tape round the perimeter of the room. Do not remove the release paper yet.

Fig 160 Unroll the carpet with one edge against the longest straight wall in the room. Peel the release paper off the tape and stick this edge down.

Fig 161 Trim off excess carpet all round after making release cuts at internal and external corners (*see* pages 34-5 for more details).

Fig 162 Stretch the carpet across the room with your feet, working from the fixed edge, and stick the opposite edge down too. Then stretch it across to the other two edges and secure them.

Laying Carpets

between floor and skirting board. Repeat the treading process from the room's centre towards the two end walls, and trim these too. Finally, remove the release paper from the tape and stick the edges down.

If you are laying **hessian-backed carpet**, start by nailing the gripper strips in place all round the room about 6mm (¼in) in from the skirting board. Then cut and fit the foam underlay so it runs right up to the strips, taping or stapling it down.

Unroll the carpet, allowing the edges to lap up the skirting boards all round, and trim it roughly to size. Make release cuts at corners as before, then start trimming to size in one corner of the room. Cut the carpet about 19mm (¾in) oversize, then use a brick bolster or similar tool to tuck the cut edge of the carpet into the gap between the gripper strip and the wall.

Now tread the carpet along each wall in turn, trimming and fixing it as you go. Finally tread the carpet across the room towards the opposite walls, and trim and fix it there too.

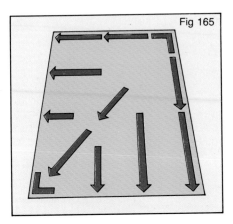

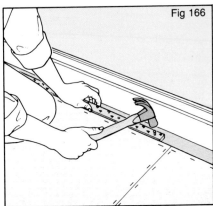

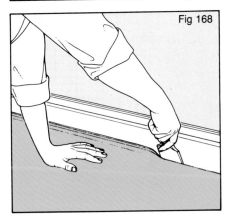

Fig 164 (*above*)   Carpet is the most luxurious floor-covering underfoot. You can team fitted carpet with loose-laid squares and rugs if you wish.

Fig 165   Fabric-backed carpet is stretched in a different way to foam-backed types, working from a corner outwards.

Fig 166   Put down foam underlay and fix gripper strips to the floor all round the room.

Fig 167   Unroll the carpet, trim roughly, make release cuts and then trim into the angle between gripper strip and skirting board.

Fig 168   Fix one corner, then stretch the carpet as shown (*see* Fig 165) and secure it by tucking the edge in place with a bolster or similar tool.

Laying Sheet Vinyl Floorcoverings

Sheet vinyl floorcoverings are one of the most difficult flooring materials to lay well, for two reasons. The material can be quite stiff, especially the thicker cushioned types, which makes room-sized sheets awkward to handle, and yet it is thin enough to leave no margin for error when trimming the edges, unlike carpet. Any gaps left by under-cutting the edges will be painfully obvious.

Sheet vinyl comes in rolls 2m (6ft 6in) and 4m (13ft) wide; buy the narrower width for small rooms such as bathrooms, and go for the larger size for kitchens and other larger rooms, so you do not have to have a seam across the room unless its dimensions exceed 4m in both directions. Some types are designed to be loose-laid, but you can avoid any risk of edges and seams curling and lifting by sticking them to the floor with double-sided adhesive tape or bands of flooring adhesive. They should not be stuck down all over the floor surface, since they will be virtually impossible to remove in the future if you decide you want to replace the floorcovering.

What to do

If you are laying sheet vinyl in a room with few or no obstacles to contend with, cut the sheet about 100mm (4in) over-large and unroll it so the edges lap up the skirting board. Make release cuts at internal and external corners, scribe the first edge if necessary and then trim the edges and tape them down (see pages 34–5 for more details).

However, by its very nature sheet vinyl is popular in rooms with the most floor-standing obstacles – kitchens, bathrooms and WCs. In this case you will get better results by making a template of the room's shape, and using this to cut out a piece of floorcovering to fit it. Lay sheets of newspaper on the floor with their edges about 25mm (1in) in from the skirting board, and tape them together (and to the floor, so they cannot move). Then use a pencil taped to a block of wood or a pair of school compasses to scribe the room's outline, as well as the outline of any obstacles, onto the paper.

What you need:
- sheet vinyl floor-covering
- sharp handyman's knife
- straightedge
- double-sided tape *or* flooring adhesive
- seam roller
- paper and tape for floor template
- scribing block
- pencil

CHECK
- that floorboards are level and secure, with protruding nail heads punched down, before you start laying the new floorcovering.

TIP
Store sheet vinyl indoors for 24 hours to allow it to acclimatize to room temperature. Warm vinyl is supple and easier to lay.
(*See also* pages 34–5)

Fig 169

Fig 169 In unobstructed rooms, unroll the sheet with one edge against the longest wall, and make release cuts to allow it to fit round obstacles and into corners. Then trim all round and stick down the edges.

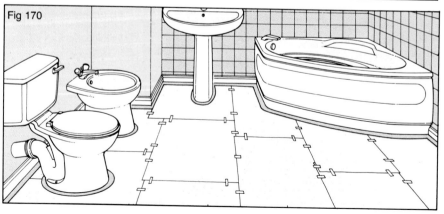

Fig 170

Fig 170 In awkwardly-shaped rooms, it is easier to make a template of the floor area than to try to cut and fit the sheet *in situ*. Tape sheets of paper together to reach to within 25mm (1in) of the skirting board.

Laying Sheet Vinyl Floorcoverings

Next, unroll the floorcovering in a larger room and place the template over it. Use the same block and pencil, or the compasses set to the same opening as before, to transcribe the outlines from the template back onto the sheet vinyl. Cut out sections of the sheet to fit round obstacles, making release cuts from the cut-out to the nearest edge of the sheet. You can now lift the sheet into place in the room where it will be laid; it should be a near-perfect fit, requiring just a sliver trimmed off here and there.

If you are worried about the accuracy of this process, draw your cutting lines a fraction outside the perimeter outline and a fraction inside the outline of any cut-outs, so you can do the final precise trimming to size when the sheet is laid in position in the room.

If you want a water-resistant floor-covering in kitchens and bathrooms and feel that fitting sheet vinyl is beyond your skills, you could contemplate laying vinyl or cork floor tiles instead (see pages 32–3 for the basic technique).

Fig 171 (*above*) Sheet vinyl is the perfect flooring for heavy-wear areas such as halls, kitchens and bathrooms.

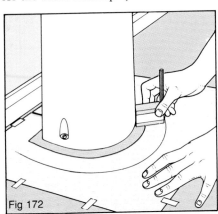

Fig 172

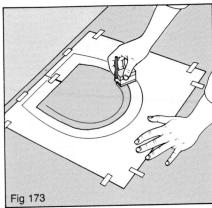

Fig 173

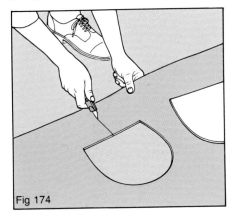

Fig 174

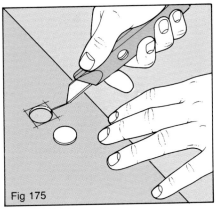

Fig 175

Fig 172 Use a block and pencil to scribe the room outline and the position of obstacles onto the template.

Fig 173 Lay the scribed template over the sheet and use the same block and pencil to scribe the room outline back onto the flooring.

Fig 174 Cut the flooring to size all round, making release cuts into enclosed cut-outs.

Fig 175 Measure and mark pipe positions, and again make cut-outs and release cuts. Then lay the sheet in place and make any small-scale adjustments needed to get a perfect fit.

Laying Ceramic and Quarry Tiles

The advantages of ceramic floor tiles make them a popular floorcovering for many areas of the home. They are easy to lay, wear well, are easy to keep clean and come in a wide range of colours and designs, so you can match almost any interior colour scheme. Perhaps their only drawback is that they are generally rather cold underfoot, especially when laid on solid concrete floors.

There is an enormous range of colours and designs available in ceramic tiles, while quarries depend on the natural clay from which they are made for any colour variation, and need sealing after laying if they are to keep their looks.

Once you've decided on the type (and design, if relevant), make a note of the tile and pack size so you can work out how many to buy. Some packs give a total coverage on the wrapping, but it's best to work out the total by accurately measuring the room size so you can calculate how many rows, containing how many tiles, will be needed. Count part tiles as whole ones, then add 5 per cent to allow for wastage.

You will also need adhesive. For ceramic tiles, buy special floor tile adhesive; there is a waterproof type for bathrooms, and a flexible type which you use when tiling on a suspended timber floor. You will need grout too, and a tile cutter, and it is worth investing in a tile file or saw if you anticipate a lot of fiddly cutting round pipes and similar obstacles.

Quarry tiles are usually laid in a mortar bed, although you can use thick-bed tile adhesive instead. It's worth hiring a heavy duty cutting jig if you have a lot of quarries to cut; ordinary cutters just aren't strong enough for the job.

Generally speaking, old floorcoverings must be lifted first. The only exception is where there are existing vinyl or cork tiles which are well stuck down; these are best left undisturbed. You can tile directly onto bare concrete.

If you want to lay ceramic tiles on a timber floor, you should always put down a layer of exterior-grade plywood first, to provide a flat and smooth surface. Use annular nails for the fixings, so there is no

What you need:
- tiles
- tile adhesive
- grout
- adhesive spreader
- grout applicator
- tile battens
- hammer and nails
- try square
- tile spacers
- spirit level
- tile cutting jig

TIP
Cover floorboards with an underlay of exterior-grade plywood to provide a firm stable base for the tiles.
(*See also* pages 32–3)

Fig 176

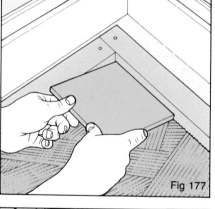

Fig 177

Fig 178

Fig 179

Fig 176 After setting out the tile pattern to your satisfaction (*see* pages 32–3) and fixing the corner guide battens, spread enough tile adhesive to cover about 1sq m (10sq ft).

Fig 177 Place the first tile in the angle between the battens and bed it down into the adhesive.

Fig 178 Continue adding tiles row by row, using spacers if necessary in between to guarantee a grout line of even width. You can remove these row by row as you work across the room.

Fig 179 Check that the tiles are laid level with each other as you proceed. Then extend the guide battens and carry on laying tiles until all the whole tiles are in place.

Laying Ceramic and Quarry Tiles

risk of the underlay lifting in the future. It is unwise to contemplate laying quarries on a timber floor, because its structure may not be strong enough to bear the extra weight without bowing.

Make sure room doors will clear the new floor surface before you start work. You will definitely have to saw or plane their bottom edges if you're laying ceramic or quarry tiles. Don't leave this until the job is finished, or you won't be able to get out of the room!

What to do

Start by setting out the tiles dry so you can find the ideal starting point and put down guide battens (see pages 32–3). Then spread some adhesive or mortar on the floor, and lay your first tile against your guide battens. Lay more tiles row by row, making sure you align the tiles in each row accurately level with each other, and use spacers to form an even grouting gap between them. Then leave the tiles overnight so the adhesive or mortar can set

before you tackle the border strip.

To ensure that the border tiles are a perfect fit, mark them using the following procedure. Place a whole tile on top of the last whole tile laid in the row. Then place another tile on top of this one, with its edge pushed hard against the skirting board, and mark a line on the middle tile against the opposite edge of the top one. The exposed part of the middle tile will then fit the gap perfectly. Cut it and lay it in place, and repeat the procedure for all the other border tiles.

Where tiles butt up to irregularly-shaped obstacles like door architraves, either make a paper template or use a shape tracer. This is a clever device consisting of a number of steel or plastic pins in a holder; you press it against the obstacle so the pins take up its profile and form a template which you can then use to mark the tile to be cut.

With all the tiles laid, remove any traces of adhesive from their surfaces and grout the gaps. Finish quarry tiles off with two or three coats of sealer.

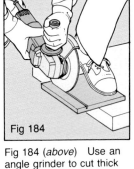

Fig 184

Fig 184 (*above*) Use an angle grinder to cut thick quarry tiles.

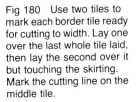

Fig 185

Fig 185 (*above*) Use a tile saw to make awkwardly-shaped cut-outs.

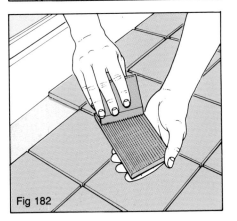

Fig 180

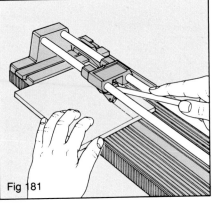

Fig 181

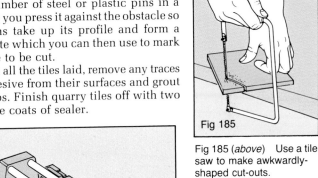

Fig 180 Use two tiles to mark each border tile ready for cutting to width. Lay one over the last whole tile laid, then lay the second over it but touching the skirting. Mark the cutting line on the middle tile.

Fig 181 Use a tile cutting jig to score and snap the tile cleanly. Thick floor tiles can be difficult to snap by hand.

Fig 182 Butter some tile adhesive onto the back of the border tile, and bed it into place.

Fig 183 When the adhesive has set, grout between the tiles and polish off excess grout with a damp cloth.

Fig 182

Fig 183

Laying Parquet Panels

If you like the look of natural timber on your floors, one solution is to lay parquet panels. These are square panels, usually either 450mm (18in) or 610mm (24in) across, made up from small fingers of wood mounted on a fabric or plastic backing sheet. They are designed to be stuck to the floor surface with special adhesive. Some are sold ready-sealed; others need two or three coats of varnish to seal the surface once the panels have been laid.

What to do

Although there is no overall design to worry about, it is still best to centre the panels as you would for other floor tiles. Use string lines to find the centre of the room, and lay the first panels to the string lines. Complete each quarter of the floor in whole panels. Then cut and fit the border strips, and pin quadrant beading to the skirting boards to hide any gaps. Some systems require the inclusion of a narrow cork expansion strip between the floor and the skirting boards, so allow for this when fitting border strips.

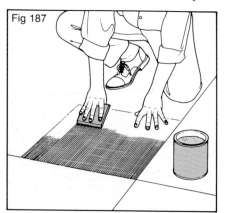

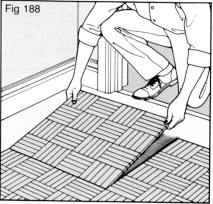

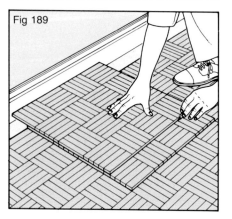

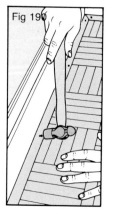

Fig 186 (*above*) Parquet panels are as easy to lay as any tile floorcovering, and come in a range of wood grains.

Fig 187 Find the mid-point of the room and spread adhesive on the floor surface.

Fig 188 Set the panel into place, using foot pressure to bed it firmly in the adhesive.

Fig 189 Use two panels to mark border strips ready for cutting to width. Lay one over the last whole panel laid, then lay the second over it but touching the skirting. Mark the cutting line on the middle panel.

Fig 190 Pin quadrant beading to the skirting board to hide any gaps. With some systems you have to fit a cork expansion strip first.

Laying Woodstrip Floors

Woodstrip floors are an alternative to parquet panels if you want a natural timber floor. The cheaper types are laminated, with a thin softwood or fibreboard backing; more expensive types are solid wood, often made up with narrow strips glued together into wider boards. Both types have tongued and grooved edges, and are usually sold pre-sealed.

You can lay woodstrip flooring directly onto an existing timber floor, but if you want to lay them over a solid concrete ground floor you must first put down a heavy gauge polythene sheet to guard against even the slightest amount of dampness swelling and warping the strips. Follow this with a felt, paper or foam underlay, as recommended by the flooring manufacturer. This cushions the underside of the strips and also helps to protect the polythene sheet from damage which could allow damp penetration.

On suspended timber floors, lay the strips at right angles to the existing floorboards. On concrete floors, it is best to lay them parallel to the longest wall.

What to do

On timber floors, fix the strips to the floor by secret-nailing through the tongue of each strip before slotting the groove of the next one over it. Drive the nails in at about 450mm (18in) intervals. Glue the last strip's grooved edge to its predecessor's tongue. Remember to leave a 12mm (½in) wide expansion gap all round the room's perimeter, covering it with quadrant beading pinned to the skirting board.

On solid floors, put down the polythene and the underlay, then lay the first strip against the wall with wedges placed between it and the skirting board to form the expansion gap. Lay subsequent boards, tapping them together tightly using an offcut to protect the projecting tongues. Some manufacturers also recommend gluing the strips together as they are laid, while others use special clips to hold the strips together. Cut the final strip down in width if necessary and glue it to its predecessor. Then fit beading all round the room to hide the expansion gap.

What you need:
- timber flooring
- fixing pins or clips
- steel tape measure
- pencil
- tenon or jigsaw
- polythene underlay (solid floors only)
- timber wedges
- edge beading

TIP
When fixing strips over an existing timber floor, run them at right angles to the existing floorboard direction.

Fig 191

Fig 191 Some woodstrip floors are designed to be laid on an existing timber floor in much the same way as putting up timber wall cladding, by secret-nailing through the tongue of each board before covering the tongue with the groove of the next board.

Others are designed for laying over any floor, solid or suspended, and have the planks held securely together with hidden clips. On solid floors, start by laying and taping the underlay sheet in place to prevent any dampness in the floor from causing the wood to swell. Then lay the first row of planks with their clips in place, adding wedges next to the skirting board to act as an expansion gap. Continue adding planks row by row until the floor is complete, then trim the underlay and cover the gap with beading.

Hanging Curtains and Blinds

Whatever type of curtain track you choose to install in your home, you are likely to be faced with the same problem every time; making a firm fixing for the track brackets into the wall just above the window opening. How easy or difficult this is depends on the type of lintel used to bridge it. In older homes stout baulks of timber were commonplace, and it is a simple matter to drive screws straight into these through the wall plaster. More modern homes will have either steel or concrete lintels. The former usually have expanded metal mesh on the inner wall surface, which is plastered over; cavity fixings are the best way of mounting the brackets here. The latter are the hardest of all to which to make fixings, because the presence of mineral aggregate within the concrete makes drilling holes for wallplugs very difficult unless a hammer drill is used.

If it proves impossible to make firm fixings immediately above the window opening, you may have to consider ceiling mounting or using a support batten.

What to do

Start by marking the positions of the fixing brackets on the wall above the window. Then test-drill the first hole; the nature of the bore dust and the sound the drill makes will tell you if you have hit wood, metal mesh or concrete.

With timber lintels, simply drill pilot holes for the screws and drive them home.

With steel lintels, drill holes through the plaster and mesh big enough to allow a cavity fixing such as a spring toggle to be inserted. Push this in far enough for the wings to spring open, then tighten the fixing screw to draw them back against the inner surface of the mesh.

With concrete lintels, use a hammer drill fitted with a masonry drill bit to make the holes, then insert wallplugs to take the fixing screws. Try drilling another hole a little way away if you cannot penetrate the lintel at your chosen spot.

If you cannot make fixings at the required bracket spacings, mount a timber batten on the wall first.

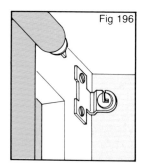

Fig 196 (*above*) Roller blinds are supported on two small end brackets, which are usually screwed to the face of the window frame.

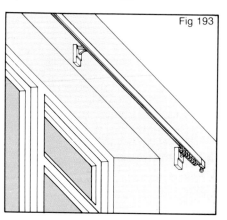

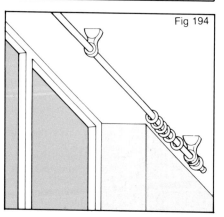

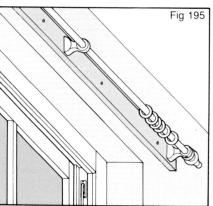

Fig 192 Most curtain poles are supported by brackets fixed to the wall above the window opening.

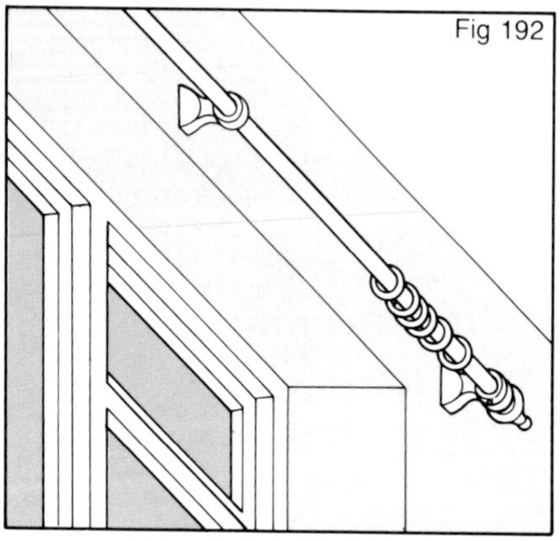

Fig 193 So are most curtain track systems. The biggest problem lies in drilling holes into concrete lintels at the required fixing positions; a hammer drill is essential.

Fig 194 An alternative is to suspend the track from brackets fixed to the ceiling.

Fig 195 If wall fixing is essential and accurate bracket positions impossible to achieve, mount a timber batten on the wall and then screw the brackets to this.

OUTDOOR JOBS

There is more to decorating the outside of your house than the physical process of slapping on the paint. Admittedly that is where the hard work lies, but deciding on colour schemes is no less important. After all, only your family and friends see your indoor decorations, while the house exterior is visible to the whole neighbourhood. Get it wrong, and everyone will think it is an eyesore.

How you decorate your house depends to a large extent on how it was built. There are certain elements – windows, doors, the woodwork at the eaves and gable ends of the roof – which are traditionally always painted or stained, and because they are really details their colour will not have a major impact on the appearance of the house. What really matters is the way the walls are decorated . . . if they need decorating at all.

Choosing Colours for Walls

While in theory you can paint your house in any colour you want, it's far better in practice to aim to make it blend in with its surroundings . . . or with the way neighbouring houses have been decorated. Start by driving or walking round the neighbourhood, noting what colours have been used and whether you find the effect pleasing. Note too what use has been made of toning or contrasting colours on exterior woodwork and other decorative features such as gutters and downpipes, balconies and outbuildings.

You can get some idea of how a particular colour scheme will look on your house by enlarging a photograph of each elevation to around 10 x 8in in size; then trace its outline and main features onto tracing paper and photocopy this to give you a number of 'blanks'. You can then colour in walls and woodwork using water colour paint or felt-tip pens to see how different colours and colour combinations will suit the building.

Apart from following any local colour traditions, there are some obvious guidelines to bear in mind. These apply particularly if you are decorating one half of a semi-detached house or any part of a row of terraced houses. Despite appearances,

each was designed as a complete building, and treating one part of it in a radically different way to its neighbours will always look unsatisfactory. It is always preferable to make wall colours blend with – if not match perfectly – those on adjacent properties, and to give the building its own touch of individuality by using stronger colours on features such as doors, windows and rainwater goods. If this can be done with the cooperation of your neighbours, so much the better.

In areas that suffer from atmospheric pollution – thankfully fewer than they were even twenty years ago – it's best to avoid light colours on walls, since they will soon become stained. Darker shades, highlighted with lighter colours on doors and windows, will stay looking cleaner for far longer.

If you have a house built of stone or brick, consider the use of paint very carefully. Some areas of the country have traditions of painting exposed masonry, but once paint is applied it completely changes the character of the building and is very difficult to remove. If painting is

Fig 197 (*above*) Decorating out of doors consists mainly of keeping woodwork in good condition, although many homes also have painted exterior walls.

Painting Your House Walls

being considered purely to disguise dirt, it may be preferable to consider some form of masonry cleaning which would reveal the original beauty of the masonry, rather than to hide it forever behind a coat of unsuitable paint.

There are two other restrictions that may affect your choice of colour. There may be restrictive covenants contained in the deeds to your property, particularly on estate-type developments where the original builder or owner was anxious to retain the overall appearance of a large number of similar properties. It may be possible to have such covenants set aside if their provisions seem totally unreasonable; if you think that yours are, contact your solicitor for advice.

The second restriction applies if you live in a Conservation Area, a National Park or an Area of Outstanding National Beauty, or if your house is a listed building. In all of these cases you will need to apply for approval from your local authority planning department before you can change the external appearance of the house.

What to do

Painting your outside walls is the biggest single decorating project you are likely to undertake, in terms of the area involved. The key to success is not to try to tackle the job in one go, but to break it down wall by wall, even using natural breaks such as rainwater downpipes to sub-divide the area still further.

Next, think about the access equipment you will need. If you plan to use a ladder, hire or buy a ladder stand-off to hold the top of the ladder clear of the eaves. It is also worth adding a tool carrier of some sort which can be fitted to the ladder to carry your paint container and painting tools, and perhaps a foot rest to ease the pain caused by standing on narrow ladder rungs for long periods. If the surrounds of your house are paved and clear of obstacles, you could consider hiring a platform tower instead; fitted with locking castors, it can then be moved along the walls as required, and will provide a comfortable and stable working platform.

What you need:
- paint
- stabilizing primer for dusty surfaces
- paint brush, roller or paint-spraying equipment
- dust sheets
- paper and masking tape
- access equipment

TIP
Try to pick a period of relatively warm and dry weather when planning your outdoor decorating. Where possible, work on surfaces out of direct sunlight, ideally those the sun has just left.

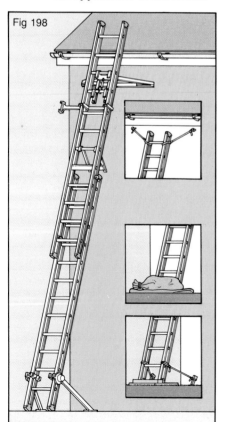

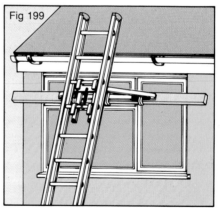

Fig 198 If you are using a ladder to reach upstairs woodwork, set it up at the correct angle with the foot of the ladder 1m (3ft) out from the wall for every 4m (12ft) of ladder height. If possible, tie it to the building at the top and secure the bottom with sandbags or pegs. Set it on a board on soft ground. Fit a ladder stay to hold the head of the ladder clear of overhanging eaves.

Fig 199 To bridge wide windows, tie a stout batten to your ladder stay so it will rest on the masonry at each side of the opening.

Fig 200 Use a pair of ladder cripples to support a scaffold board so you can work over projecting bay windows.

Painting House Walls

Start work by preparing the surface, brushing off any loose material and treating mould growth with a fungicide. Apply a coat of stabilizing primer if the surface is at all dusty.

You can apply the paint by brush, roller or spray. Brushing is the slowest method, but you can speed things up by using a soft-bristled banister brush and a paint tray instead of a paintbrush and kettle. Rollers are ideal for smooth and lightly textured surfaces, but cannot cope with heavy textures such as pebbledash. Spraying the paint on is the quickest solution, despite the time needed to mask off doors, windows and downpipes, and will cope easily with the heaviest textures. When you hire the equipment, tell your supplier what sort of paint you are applying; you need special equipment to spray paints with added fillers, which many masonry paints contain.

Try to follow the progress of the sun round the house as you work, painting each wall after the sun has just left it so its surface is warm and dry.

Fig 201 (*above*) Use masonry paint containing a fungicide for all exterior brick and stonework.

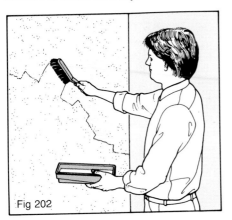

Fig 202

Fig 203

Fig 202 You can apply paint quickly to textured surfaces using a soft banister brush instead of an ordinary paintbrush.

Fig 203 Use a roller with an extension pole on smooth rendering.

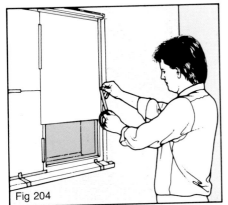

Fig 204

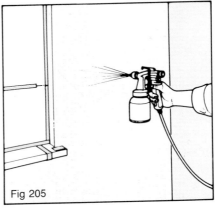

Fig 205

Fig 204 Alternatively, use a spray gun to apply the paint – ideal for heavily-textured surfaces such as pebbledash. First mask windows, downpipes and other surfaces with paper and masking tape.

Fig 205 Use the correct gun for the paint type you are applying, and spray the paint on evenly area by area.

Painting Outdoor Woodwork

When it comes to painting things like doors, windows, fascias and bargeboards, gutters and downpipes, your choice of colour can, within reason, be entirely personal. If your walls are of dark masonry or are painted in a deep shade, you will get a more pleasing contrast by painting architectural details in white or a lighter colour, while white or pastel walls look much more attractive with strong colours on the details. As with your walls, use other buildings in your area as a guide to choosing the most pleasing colour combination. On many styles of house you can enhance the impact of door and window openings by painting their reveals or surrounds in the same colour as the woodwork itself. If white is used in this situation, you get the added benefit of having more light reflected in through small window openings.

Remember too that you can liven up the exterior of your house by adding small 'spots' of colour in the form of window boxes, hanging flower baskets and even wooden window shutters.

What to do

There is no technical difference between painting wood and metalwork out of doors and doing it indoors. However, you have to contend with two minor inconveniences; having to work off a ladder to paint things at or above first-floor level, and having to keep an eye on the weather. You can make working up a ladder more comfortable by fitting it with a stand-off to hold the ladder head away from the wall, plus a tool carrier and foot rest. As far as the weather is concerned, you obviously should not start work if rain is forecast or the weather is generally cold and damp; the latter conditions will prevent the paint from drying properly. The ideal conditions are a warm, dry day when you can follow the sun round the building as you work.

On the plus side, there is the unspoken agreement among home decorators that you do not have to take quite so much care to get perfect results out of doors as you would indoors, so you can work faster.

Prepare surfaces as you would indoors,

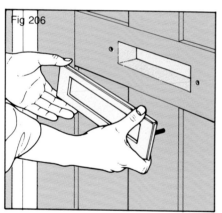

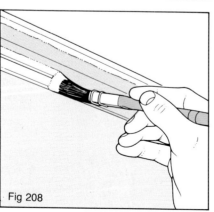

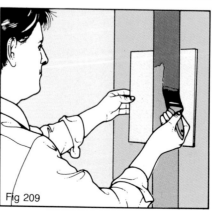

Fig 206 Remove door furniture before starting to paint exterior doors.

Fig 207 Unless you have a very steady hand, use masking tape round windows to ensure a neat finish. Position it so the paint will cover the edge of the glass by about 3mm (⅛in) and prevent water from penetrating behind the putty or glazing bead.

Fig 208 Ensure that paint fills the angle between paint and glass. Remove the tape when the paint is touch dry.

Fig 209 Use a cardboard mask when painting features such as downpipes, to keep paint from spoiling the wall surfaces.

Painting Outdoor Woodwork

removing flaking paint and priming bare surfaces where necessary. If you have to strip paint back to bare wood, use a hot air gun or blowlamp, taking care near windows not to let the heat crack the glass. Look out for patches of rotten wood, and cut out any that you find, patching the damage with exterior-quality filler or new wood as appropriate. On metal, wire-brush off any rust and treat the surface with a rust inhibitor before repainting it.

Remove things like door furniture before you start painting, and use masking tape on windows to get a neat paint edge that runs onto the glass surface by about 3mm (⅛in) all round; this prevents rainwater from running down behind the putty and causing rot in the glazing bars. Use a cardboard mask behind things like downpipes to keep paint off the wall surface.

Paint doors and windows in the same sequence as for indoors (see pages 39 and 40 for more details). Wedge doors open until the paint is touch-dry, and put 'WET PAINT' warning signs up where they will be clearly visible to the rest of the family.

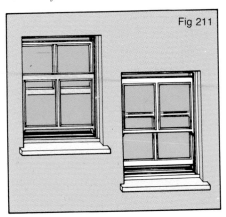

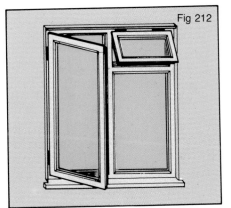

Fig 210 (*above*) The architectural style of your home will dictate how much painting work is involved. Some people are luckier than others!

Fig 211 To paint a sash window, start by reversing the sashes so you can paint the top of the lower sash and the top of the channels in which the outer sash slides. When the paint is touch dry, reverse the sashes to complete the painting process.

Fig 212 Paint opening casements first, then their rebates, finishing off with the frame.

Fig 213 Wedge exterior doors open while you paint them. On panelled and glazed doors, tackle the panels or glazing bars first, then the rails and stiles.

Using Stain, Varnish and Preservative

Although paint is still the most popular material for decorating the exterior woodwork of our homes, there has been a rapid growth in recent years in the use of wood stains as an alternative finish (and a corresponding decline in the use of varnish). The reason for this is that most people dislike carrying out the regular maintenance work needed to keep outdoor paintwork in good condition, and modern exterior wood stains provide a decorative finish that is far simpler to maintain.

This is thanks to the development of a formulation which prevents water penetration while still allowing moisture vapour to pass through the coating; such stains are described as being microporous. Microporous paints – in fact, heavily pigmented stains – are also available. The only drawback with both products is that they must be applied to bare wood if they are to perform as designed; they convey no benefit if applied over existing finishes.

The other product you will need for outdoor maintenance is wood preservative, to be used on fences, gates and outbuildings.

What to do

If you are applying an exterior wood stain to bare wood, simply brush it on to the surface working parallel to the grain direction. Add a second coat for complete protection. Where the woodwork already has a stained finish in need of redecoration, simply wash down the surface to remove dirt and dust, and apply a fresh coat.

If you prefer the high gloss finish of exterior varnish, pay particular care to the surface preparation. Degrease new wood thoroughly, and if you are re-varnishing an existing finish strip off any cracked or flaking material and sand the surface to provide a good key for the new coat. Avoid using varnish on surfaces that are exposed to direct sunlight for long periods; the ultra-violet rays in sunlight will cause early failure of the film.

You can apply preservative to fences, gates and outbuildings by brush or spray. When spraying, take care to keep the spray off plants unless you are using a non-toxic preservative.

What you need:
- wood stain
- wood preservative
- paintbrush *or* paint-spraying equipment

CHECK
- that you use a horticultural grade of preservative on wood near plants
- that over-spray will not be harmful if applying preservative with a spray gun.

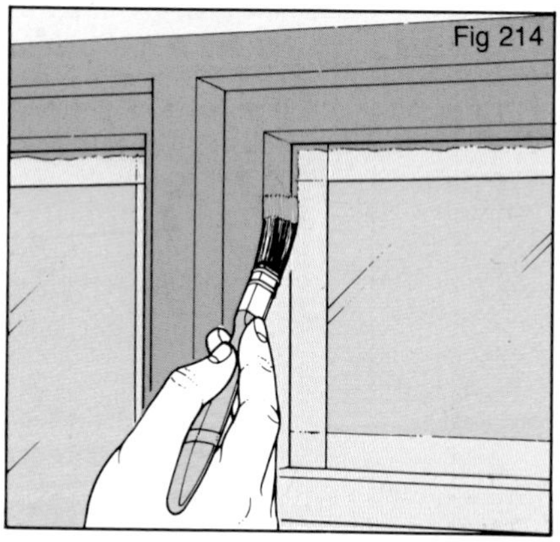

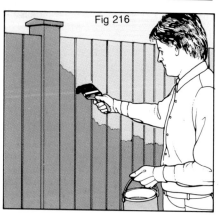

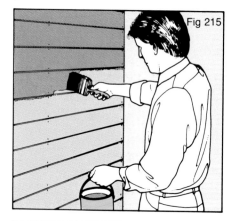

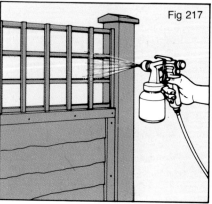

Fig 214 Exterior wood stains are a popular alternative to paint on many new homes, since they wear better and are easier to recoat when redecorating. Simply wash the surface and apply a fresh coat.

Fig 215 Treat timber outbuildings regularly with preservative to keep them in good condition.

Fig 216 Timber fencing also needs regular preservative treatment to prevent rot. Use water-based types that will not harm plant life if vegetation is nearby.

Fig 217 You can spray preservatives onto awkward-to-treat surfaces such as trellis, but take care that overspray does not blow onto other surfaces.

PREPARATION & REPAIRS

Decorating is a very positive type of home improvement; by definition, what you finish up with is bound to look better than what was there before, unless you have managed to ignore all the advice given in this book and have made a complete mess of whatever you are tackling. However, good results are not automatically achieved; any successful decorating project consists of one-tenth surface gloss and nine-tenths hidden but nevertheless essential preparation.

In this chapter you will find information on removing existing decorations, advice on how to prepare surfaces for whatever new finish you propose to give them, and also a few words about the sort of running repairs you will often have to carry out to various surfaces between removing the old and applying the new.

Off with the Old

If your idea of home decorating consists merely of washing down the woodwork and putting some more emulsion paint on the walls about once every five years, you will not be over-concerned with removing old decorations. However, many home decorators prefer to change their interior decorations frequently, and anyone who is moving house is likely to be faced with the prospect of completely redecorating the property from top to bottom; someone else's idea of good taste rarely coincides with your own.

Most people are familiar with what is involved in removing old paint or wall-coverings. However, a wide range of other decorating materials have begun to be used in the home in recent years, and you may well want to be rid of things as diverse as tiles, wall fabrics, timber cladding and textured finishes. The problems these can pose act as a useful reminder to every home decorator contemplating a change of scene; will what I am finding so easy to put up now be difficult to remove in five year's time when I am sick of the sight of it? Everyone knows someone who is still struggling with the remains of those hideous polystyrene tiles everyone stuck on their ceilings twenty years ago, and not everyone loves cork wall tiles or Artex!

Be Prepared!

Preparation is the boring, messy time-consuming and thoroughly unenjoyable part of home decorating. However, time spent doing it thoroughly and properly brings its own reward; paint flows on effortlessly, there are no lumps and bumps to spoil the look of your expensive new wallcovering, and the final effect looks thoroughly professional. Skimp on your preparation and it shows.

The biggest enemies of paint and other liquid decorations are dirt, grease and dust. Yet many decorators believe you can simply paint over an existing surface and expect the paint to hide everything, and do not even bother to dust surfaces first. As far as hanging wallcoverings are concerned, thorough preparation of the wall surfaces results in greater ease of positioning of the individual lengths as well as improved long-term adhesion.

Make Do and Mend

There will be occasions when you do not have the time or the money to redecorate, and are faced instead with making do with what you already have. Knowing how to patch damage and make repairs will at least help make the best of a bad job.

Fig 218 (*above*) Most decorating jobs are nine-tenths preparation and one-tenth application. Skimp on the former, and the results will always be disappointing.

Stripping Paint

Repainting is one of the quickest ways of sprucing up surfaces around the house. As far as walls are concerned, you can within reason apply layer after layer of paint without ever having to remove it, and a painted wall is the perfect base for many other decorative finishes too. But paint on woodwork and metalwork cannot be allowed to build up for ever. On doors and windows it eventually reaches such a thickness that it causes moving parts to jam in their frames; on any surface the build-up also gradually highlights imperfections in the layers below the surface, and superficial damage exposes unsightly chips of long-forgotten colours. There comes a time when you need to strip everything back to bare wood and start again.

You can do this in one of two ways: by heating the paint film or by applying special chemicals to it. Both methods soften the film so it can be scraped off, but each has advantages and disadvantages. Which method you choose will depend on what you are stripping and how you want to redecorate it.

What to do

If you have large areas of wood to strip and you intend to repaint the surface again afterwards, heat stripping is the best method to choose. A blowlamp is the traditional tool for the job, but modern electric hot air strippers and gas guns do the job just as well with far less risk of burning the house down. Their main drawback is that you must use them with care when stripping paint near glass, since the heat can crack it. Most electric and gas guns come with a heat shield which helps to deflect the stream of hot air from the glass. To use one you simply play the hot air over the paint until it begins to blister and lift, then scrape it off with a stripping knife or shavehook. Have a tin or similar heat-proof container handy so you can deposit the scrapings in it instead of dropping them on the floor.

You *can* use a hot air gun to strip wood which you want to stain or varnish, but you have to be careful not to char the wood as you strip the paint. A better bet in

What you need:
- blowlamp *or*
- hot air gun *or*
- chemical paint stripper
- stripping knife
- shave hook
- paint brush
- container for stripper
- water or white spirit for neutralizing stripper

TIP
Don't use heat stripping on metal, since it conducts the heat away as fast as you apply it. Instead, use chemical strippers or have large items sand-blasted.

Fig 219

Fig 220

Fig 221

Fig 222

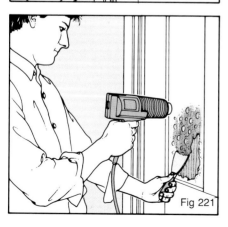

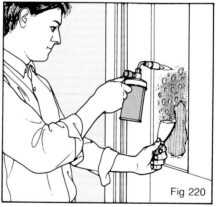

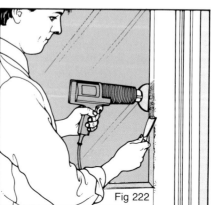

Fig 219 A blowlamp is the traditional tool for stripping solvent-based paints – gloss and eggshell. It is cheap to run and can be used anywhere, but tends to char the wood and can start fires if used carelessly. To use one, start by playing a soft flame over the paint until it bubbles up.

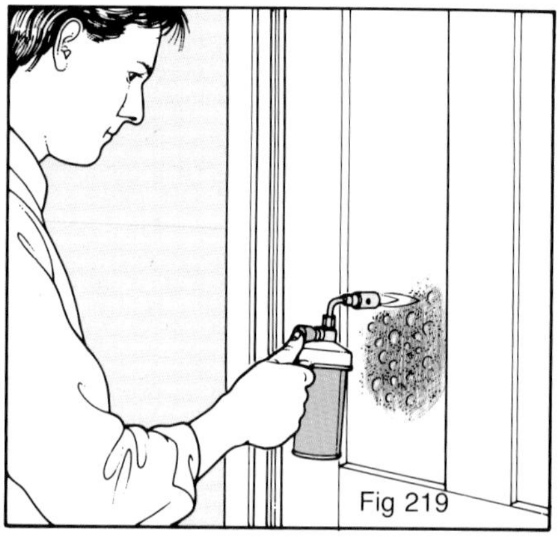

Fig 220 Then use a scraper to lift the paint film, applying more heat if necessary.

Fig 221 An electric hot air gun works in the same way as a blowlamp, but the hot air stream leads to less charring.

Fig 222 You can use a hot air gun for stripping paint near glass if you fit a heat deflector.

Stripping Paint

this case is to use a chemical paint stripper. Most liquid strippers are based on a chemical called methylene chloride and come as either a runny liquid or a thicker gel; always use the latter on vertical surfaces. The alternative is a stripper based on caustic soda, usually sold as a thick paste which adheres to vertical surfaces better than either a gel or liquid type. You simply brush the stripper onto the surface, leave it for a while to soften the paint and then scrape it off. Where there are several layers to strip, you may need a second application of stripper to get right back to bare wood. You then have to rinse off the surface to ensure that no traces are left to attack your new finish; you usually use water for this, but some need rinsing with white spirit.

Caustic soda strippers are also used by commercial firms who offer a door or furniture-stripping service. This is not expensive and can be a speedy way of getting a batch of doors stripped. However, dipping furniture can cause joints to open up, so do not send valuable pieces to be stripped by this method.

Fig 223 (*above*) Use a hot air gun for stripping outdoor paintwork too, but take care to keep the tool's lead out of the hot air stream.

Fig 224

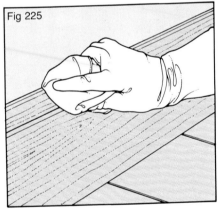

Fig 225

Fig 224 Chemical strippers are ideal for stripping surfaces you want to stain or varnish. Brush them on and give them time to work, then scrape off the softened paint.

Fig 225 Neutralize the stripper with water or white spirit as directed and then sand the wood.

Fig 226 Immerse paint-stained fittings in a jar of liquid stripper.

Fig 227 Use liquid strippers near glass to avoid the risk of heat cracking it. A shavehook will cope with intricate mouldings.

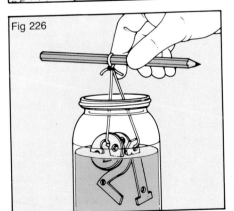

Fig 226

Fig 227

Stripping Wallcoverings

You can in general paint over old paint, but you cannot hang a new wallcovering successfully over an existing one. There are two reasons for this. Firstly, the existing wallpaper may begin to lift from the wall as the paste from the paper you are hanging soaks into it, causing at best localized blistering and at worst total failure. Secondly, wallpaper paste simply will not stick to the surface of many modern plastic-coated wallcoverings. The golden rule is always to strip back to the bare wall surface underneath first.

As with stripping paint, there are several different methods you can use to remove old wallcoverings. Which you choose depends on what you are stripping, but all work on broadly the same principle of softening the water-soluble paste so you can scrape off the wallcovering with a stripping knife. However, there are two types of wallcovering which are stripped differently. With vinyl wallcoverings, you peel off the printed plastic layer dry first, then soak and strip the paper backing. Novamura simply peels off dry.

What to do

To strip **printed uncoated wallpapers** and the paper backing of vinyl wallcoverings, simply soak the paper surface with water from a sponge or a garden spray gun and leave it to soak in for a few minutes. You can improve the rate of water penetration by adding a little washing-up liquid or a proprietary liquid wallpaper stripper to it, and warm water works better than cold. Then use a broad stripping knife to scrape the paper off, taking care not to gouge out the plaster as you hack away at the stubborn bits. Finally, rinse the wall down with clean water to remove any nibs of paper and the remains of the old paste.

If you are stripping walls by the soak-and-scrape method, it is wise to turn off the electricity supply in case water finds its way into wiring accessories such as light switches and power points. If this is not possible, tape polythene over them with water-resistant tape.

To strip **washable and painted papers**, you need to use some means of penetrating

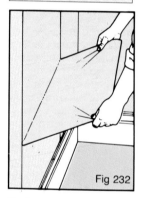

Fig 232

Fig 232 (*above*) Strip vinyls by peeling off the plastic surface layer dry, then soak and scrape off the porous backing paper.

Fig 228

Fig 229

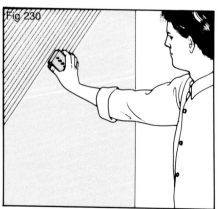

Fig 230

Fig 231

Fig 228   To strip ordinary wallpapers, soak them with water using a sponge or a garden spray gun.

Fig 229   To strip washable papers, first cross-hatch the plastic surface with the edge of your stripping knife to allow the water to penetrate, or . . .

Fig 230   Use a serrated scraper to achieve the same effect.

Fig 231   Then scrape the softened paper from the wall, sponging stubborn areas again as you work your way across the wall surface.

the waterproof surface layer so the water can get at the paste. You can do this by cross-hatching the surface with the corner of your stripping knife, or by using a serrated scraper. However, both methods are laborious and time-consuming if you have large areas to strip.

A far quicker solution is to hire a steam wallpaper stripper. This has a water reservoir which is electrically heated, and a hose which carries the resulting steam to a perforated plate which you press against the wall surface. This forces the steam into the wallcovering, softening the paste and allowing the paper to be scraped off. As you get used to using it, you will find that you can steam one area, then scrape it while steaming the next one. Again, rinse the wall down with clean water when you have finished the stripping. You can use the steam stripper to strip wallcoverings from ceilings, and to remove a wide range of speciality wallcoverings such as hessian.

Once you have stripped the wall, use interior filler to repair any gouges, holes and cracks in the plaster surface.

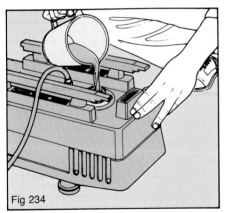

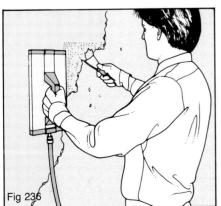

Fig 233 (*above*) This small steam stripper closely resembles a steam iron, and is an inexpensive alternative to a hired steam stripper.

Fig 234 To use a hired steam stripper, first fill the water reservoir and switch on the power.

Fig 235 Press the steaming plate to the wall for a few seconds, then lift it away and test to see whether the wallcovering is soft enough to strip.

Fig 236 Carry on stripping, steaming the next area while scraping paper off the one you have just steamed.

Fig 237 Finish the job by re-steaming and then stripping any stubborn areas of wallcovering.

Removing Textured Finishes

Textured finishes for ceilings (and to a lesser extent, walls) have been popular for many years. Apart from giving the surface a three-dimensional appearance which is often elaborately patterned, they are also excellent at covering up minor blemishes such as hairline cracks. There are two types of product used to create these textures. The first is a powder which is mixed with water to a creamy consistency, while the second is really a thickened emulsion paint called, appropriately, textured paint. Both are brushed onto the surface being decorated, and are then textured with a variety of tools (see page 43).

If you have this type of finish in your home, you can give it a quick facelift by painting it with emulsion or solvent-based paint after washing the surface down to remove air-borne dirt, grease and tar stains from cigarettes. However, heavily textured types can be difficult to clean, and you may decide that another form of decoration would be more appropriate. You have two choices; to remove the finish or to cover it up (see Tip).

What to do

The first thing you must do is to try to establish whether you have a powder-type coating such as Artex, or a textured emulsion paint. The best way of testing this is to hold the spout of a boiling electric kettle near the surface for a minute or two so you can see whether the steam softens the material. If it does, it is Artex or a similar compound; if it does not it is a textured emulsion paint.

You can strip the former type fairly quickly using a steam wallpaper stripper, used just as if you were stripping wallpaper. To remove the latter you need to use a special textured paint remover; ordinary paint strippers will not work.

Strip the room and put down dust sheets to protect floorcoverings. Make sure you are wearing safety goggles to guard against getting splashes of the stripper in your eyes, and add some protective headgear such as an old cap too. Then brush on the stripper, allow it to soften the paint and scrape it off with a stripping knife.

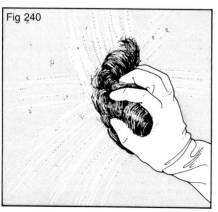

Fig 238 You can strip textured emulsion paint with a special chemical paint stripper. Brush it on generously and leave it to soften the paint.

Fig 239 Then scrape the paint off, depositing the scrapings in a rigid container. Wear gloves, and also safety goggles if stripping a ceiling.

Fig 240 Finally, scrub the surface down with wire wool to remove any remaining flecks of paint.

Fig 241 The best way of removing traditional Artex finishes is to use a steam wallpaper stripper. This softens the compound so you can scrape it off. NEVER try to use abrasives to remove this material; many older types contained asbestos.

Removing Tiles and Cladding

There are two wall decorations which you may have and may want no longer; ceramic tiles, and decorative timber cladding. Both are among the more permanent decorations around, and removing them will involve a lot more hard work, disruption and mess than stripping paint or wallpaper.

What to do: Ceramic Tiles

The only way of removing ceramic tiles from wall surfaces is to use brute force, literally chopping them off with a brick bolster and club hammer. How easy or difficult this is depends on how well the tiles were originally put up; all you can do is hope they were a bodged job!

Start work at a corner or open edge, driving the edge of the bolster down behind the edge of the tile. Some tiles may split off in one piece; you will have to chip others off bit by bit. Try to remove as much of the old tile adhesive as you can at the same time. Do not worry if some of the plaster pulls away as you work; simply fill the damaged areas later.

What to do: Timber Cladding

To remove individual planks which are usually nailed to wall battens, first remove any perimeter trims. Then try to prise away a board at one side of the wall. The last one fixed will probably have had its tongue removed and will be held in place by pins punched through its face, so should come away fairly easily. Once that has been removed, use an old chisel to lever the rest of the planks away from the wall battens one by one. Finally, remove the wall battens and make good any damage to the wall surface.

To remove old wallboards, check first whether they sound hollow; this indicates they are fixed to battens and can be prised off in the same way as individual planks. If they sound solid they have probably been stuck in place with bands of adhesive. Try to lever an edge away, then use a bolster and club hammer to 'chisel' the board off the wall. You may find that a hot air gun will help soften the bands of adhesive so you can scrape them off.

Fig 242 To strip an area of old tiles, try to start work at a corner. Drive a brick bolster behind the edge tiles and lever them off – either whole if you are lucky, or otherwise in sections.

Fig 243 Carry on working across the wall in this way, trying to remove as much tile adhesive as possible at the same time. Unless you are prepared to replaster the wall when you have finished, do not expect it to be smooth enough for paint or wallpaper.

Fig 244 To remove tongue-and-groove timber cladding, start by prising off the skirting board and any decorative beading round the edges.

Fig 245 Then start at one side of the area and lever the boards away from their battens with a hammer and chisel or a crowbar. Finally prise off the wall battens and make good any damage.

Preparing Woodwork for Redecorating

The average home contains a lot of woodwork which traditionally has a paint or varnish finish. Giving this a fresh top coat is one of the commonest decorating jobs, and getting good results depends as much on the quality of the preparation as on your skill with a paintbrush.

What to do: Existing Paintwork

Start by washing the painted surfaces down with strong detergent or sugar soap to remove surface dirt, greasy finger marks and the like. Rinse off with clean water and allow them to dry. Then sand the surfaces with fine wet-and-dry abrasive paper used wet; don't use ordinary glasspaper, which gets clogged with paint. Use fine wire wool on curved surfaces. This will remove the surface gloss and key the surface ready to receive the new coating. Finally, wipe over the surfaces with a clean lint-free cloth dipped in white spirit, to remove paint dust and any remaining finger marks. Apply the new coating immediately.

What to do: Bare Wood

If you are painting bare wood – a new door, replacement skirting boards and the like – for the first time, start by sanding the wood surface down with fine and then flour grade abrasive until the surface feels perfectly smooth to the touch. Then wipe away the dust with a cloth dipped in white spirit, and apply the first coat of your paint or varnish system.

With paint, start with a coat of wood primer followed by an undercoat and top coat – the traditional three-layer paint system. Alternatively, use a quick-drying primer/undercoat and a top coat, or wood primer followed by a self-undercoating gloss top coat.

With varnish, thin the first coat with about 10 per cent white spirit to help it to penetrate the bare wood, and apply it with a lint-free cloth pad. Brush on the second and third coats at full strength.

Always allow each coat to dry thoroughly before applying the next, and sand each one lightly to remove any dust specks.

Fig 246

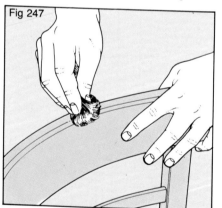

Fig 247

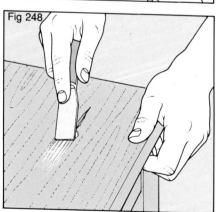

Fig 248

Fig 249

Fig 246   If you are simply repainting existing paintwork, sand the surface lightly with wet-and-dry abrasive paper to provide a key for the new paint, then wash it down to remove grease and dust. If you have stripped paint back to bare wood, use glasspaper instead.

Fig 247   Smooth curved surfaces with wire wool.

Fig 248   Fill splits and dents with wood stopper, using a colour close to that of the wood if it is to be stained or varnished. Leave the repair slightly proud of the wood surface.

Fig 249   When the stopper has dried hard, sand it down so it is flush with the surface of the surrounding wood.

Preparing Walls and Ceilings for Redecorating

As with woodwork, the key to successful decoration of wall and ceiling surfaces lies in thorough preparation. What you do depends on the existing condition of the surface, and on how you want to decorate (or redecorate) it.

What to do: Existing Paint

If your walls and ceilings are painted at present and you plan to repaint them, start by washing the surfaces down with strong detergent or sugar soap to remove dirt and grease. Use a 'squeegee' mop to make washing ceilings easier. Rinse off with clean water and allow to dry. Then fill any cracks and holes with interior filler, leaving the filler slightly proud so you can sand it down flush when set.

What to do: Stripped Surfaces

If you have removed old wallcoverings, always wash the surface down thoroughly with water to remove the remains of the old paste and any nibs of backing paper.

If the wall is bare plaster and you intend to rehang another wallcovering, all you need to do is to attend to any major cracks or defects. If you want to paint it, fill blemishes carefully and then thin the first coat of emulsion so it will brush on more easily. Follow this with one or two full-strength coats as necessary.

What to do: Fresh Plaster

If you are planning to decorate freshly-plastered surfaces, stick to emulsion paint or plain wallpaper (not washables or vinyls) so the plasterwork can continue to dry out through the decorations. Brush off any efflorescence – white powdery surface deposits caused by dissolved minerals being left behind on the plaster surface as it dries out – and remove any nibs to leave a perfectly smooth surface. If you are using emulsion, dilute the first coat of paint. If you are paper-hanging, brush on a coat of size – diluted wallpaper paste – to cut the surface porosity so you can slide the wallpaper easily into position.

> **What you need:**
> - sugar soap or strong detergent
> - bucket and sponge or squeegee
> - multi-purpose primer
> - paint brush
> - spirit level
> - steel tape measure
> - pencil
> - lining paper
> - paper-hanging tools

Fig 250

Fig 251

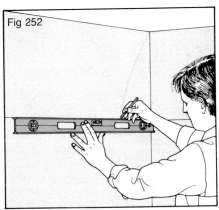

Fig 252

Fig 253

Fig 250 Always wash down painted wall and ceiling surfaces with strong detergent or sugar soap to remove dirt and grease, whether you are repainting or paper-hanging. Use a floor squeegee to reach high ceilings.

Fig 251 If you have removed old distemper or wallcoverings and have exposed bare plaster or plasterboard, seal the porous surface with a multi-purpose primer before you start to redecorate it.

Fig 252 Cross-line wall surfaces that are crazed or uneven with lining paper if you are hanging another wallcovering. Start by drawing a horizontal line on the wall surface.

Fig 253 Hang the paper to this line, unfurling the concertina folds as you brush the paper into place. Take care not to overlap the joints between lengths.

Preparing Metalwork for Redecorating

Inside the house, the metal surfaces you are most likely to want to paint are the central heating radiators and any exposed heating or water supply pipework. Out of doors, you may have cast-iron gutters and downpipes, steel window frames, iron railings and gates to attend to.

What to do: Indoors

If radiator and pipe surfaces have been painted already, wash them down with detergent or sugar soap to remove dirt and grease, rinse them with clean water and key the paint surface with wet-and-dry abrasive paper used wet. Finally, wipe over with a cloth moistened in white spirit, and apply a fresh coat of paint. If you find any rust spots on your radiators, wire-brush back to bare metal and apply a rust inhibitor before spot-priming the affected area and repainting.

If you have bare copper pipework, use fine wire wool to remove any surface discoloration and leave the metal bright and clean. Then degrease it with white spirit and immediately apply a coat of zinc chromate or zinc phosphate metal primer, followed by one or two top coats of gloss or eggshell paint as preferred.

What to do: Outdoors

Rust is the biggest enemy of outdoor metalwork, and you will be lucky if you do not find any. Use a wire brush to strip rust back to bare metal, then apply a rust inhibitor followed by a coat of calcium plumbate primer and then one or two top coats of exterior gloss paint. Alternatively, if the rust is mainly superficial you can simply apply a coat of rust-inhibiting exterior metal paint straight over it. This is an ideal treatment for fiddly exterior metalwork such as railings and gates.

If you have cast-iron gutters, do not neglect the inside surfaces where rust can eat away unseen. Remove debris and wash out the gutters with clean water from a garden hose. Allow them to dry, then brush on a liberal coat of black bituminous paint to seal and protect the surface.

What you need:
- wire wool
- power drill and wire cup or wheel brush
- rust inhibitor
- metal primer
- rust-inhibiting paint
- paint brush

CHECK
- that rust spots on radiators are completely removed, and that there are no leaks from seams or pinholes. If there are, replace the radiator before a major leak occurs.

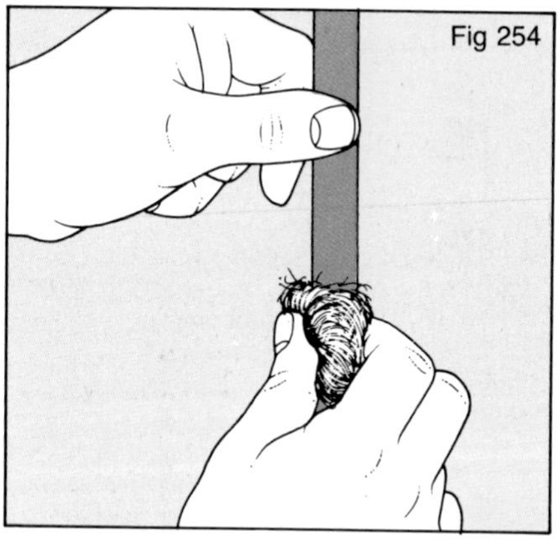

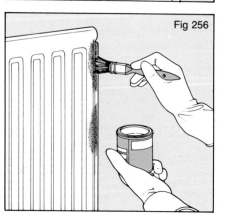

Fig 254   Rub down bare metal surfaces such as copper plumbing and heating pipes with wire wool, then apply a coat of metal primer.

Fig 255   Use a wire brush to remove rust from metalwork out of doors, then apply rust inhibitor followed by metal primer.

Fig 256   Use rust inhibitor to tackle small patches of rust on indoor surfaces such as radiators.

Fig 257   To save preparation time out of doors, simply treat rusty metalwork with a coat of rust-inhibiting metal paint.

Repairing Damaged Wallcoverings

Some wallcoverings, notably vinyl types, are surprisingly tough and can withstand quite a lot of rough treatment. However, even a vinyl wallcovering cannot withstand the sort of damage likely to be caused by the impact of carelessly-moved furniture or collisions with children's wheeled toys. The resulting damage is usually at best a tear in the wallcovering, and perhaps damage to the plaster behind too. Until you next redecorate, the best way of disguising such damage is by patching it with an offcut.

You may also find as time goes by that the seams or corners of individual lengths of wallcovering are beginning to lift away from the wall surface, and unless these are attended to they can easily be torn right away from the wall. Prompt action can soon stick them back into place.

Another problem you may encounter are blisters that refuse to pull out after a new wallcovering has been hung, leaving a visibly raised area. This is generally the result of careless pasting leaving a dry area on the back of the length.

What to do

If damage to the surface of the wall has left a jagged tear in the wallcovering, try to stick the torn piece back in place with a little wallpaper paste or a general-purpose household adhesive.

If part of the wallcovering is actually missing and you have some spare paper, tear back the edges of the damaged area to leave feathered edges, slightly larger than the damaged area. Feather-edge the patch and stick it in place, using paste for ordinary papers and special overlap adhesive on washables and vinyls. If you have no spare paper, you may be able to tear off enough material for the repair from behind some fitted furniture or an inconspicuous corner of the room.

Stick raised seams and corners back down by lifting them with a knife and brushing in paste or overlap adhesive, then press them down with a seam roller.

Cure blisters by making two right-angled cuts across their centre, folding back the tongues and brushing in some fresh paste.

What you need:
- wallpaper paste
- offcut of wallcovering
- knife
- overlap adhesive
- seam roller

TIP
Always keep a short length of any wallcovering you use stored in a file, so you can patch small areas of damage when they occur.

Fig 258

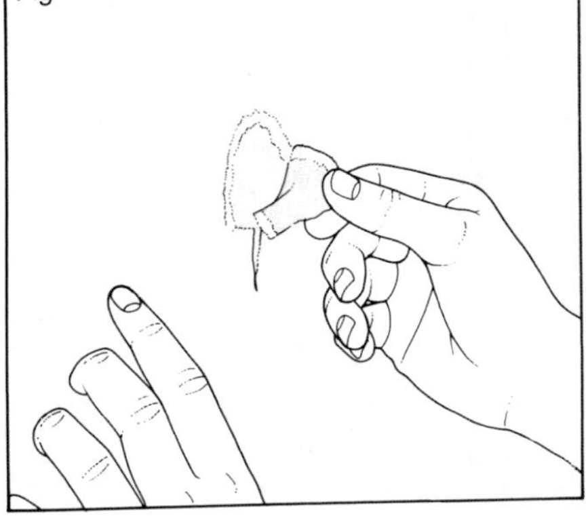

Fig 259

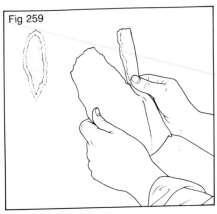

Fig 260

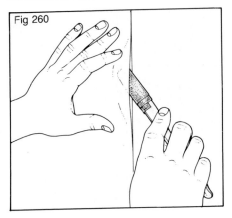

Fig 261

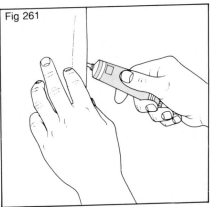

Fig 258   Where wallpaper has been torn, stick the tear back if possible with a little wallpaper paste. If this is not possible and you have saved an offcut of the original paper, tear the damaged part off carefully to leave a smoothly feathered edge.

Fig 259   Feather the edges of a matching patch, paste it and stick it into place over the hole, matching the pattern as best you can. Use overlap adhesive to stick the patch on vinyl or washable papers.

Fig 260   If seams are lifting, work a knife beneath them to raise them a little more.

Fig 261   Then squeeze in a little overlap adhesive and press the seam back into place. Use a seam roller unless the paper is embossed.

Repairing Damaged Tiles

Ceramic wall and floor tiles are among the most durable of all materials, but both can be cracked by an accidental impact and wall tiles in particular may be cracked or lifted from the wall surface by movement in the wall structure. This is especially common where the tiles have been stuck to a stud partition wall in a room with high humidity such as a bathroom. Old tiles may also suffer from crazed glazing, which looks unsightly and can be un-hygienic too. The solution is to remove the affected tiles and replace them, with matching tiles if these are available or with as close a match as you can reasonably achieve otherwise.

Two other problems often affect tiled areas. The first is gradual discoloration of the grout lines, which can mar the area's appearance even if the tile surfaces are clean and sound. The second is the dis-coloration of beads of silicone sealant used to waterproof the junction between the tiles and another surface such as a bath. Here the solutions are to re-grout the tiles and to replace the sealant.

What to do

To remove a single tile that is cracked, work from the centre towards its edges. For wall tiles, use a cold chisel (or even an old wood chisel) to prise the pieces of tile away from the wall. For floor tiles, use a brick bolster. In both cases, take care not to damage the surrounding tiles. Then chip away as much of the old tile adhesive as you can. Butter tile adhesive onto the back of the replacement tile and bed it in place level with its neighbours, then grout round it.

If the tile is loose but still whole, try to lever it away from the wall by inserting a chisel blade under its edge. Then scrape old adhesive off the wall or floor surface, and soak the tile to soften any adhesive stuck to its back so you can carefully scrape that off too. Rebed it with fresh adhesive as before.

To re-grout tiles, rake out the old grout with an old screwdriver or similar tool and apply fresh grout to the joint lines, finishing them off neatly.

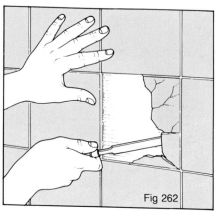

Fig 262

Fig 263

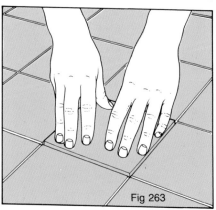

Fig 263

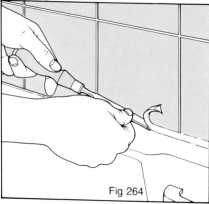

Fig 264

Fig 262 Where an individual wall tile is cracked or crazed, break it up with judicious use of a hammer, then lever out the bits with an old chisel or similar tool. Then scrape off as much of the old adhesive and grout as possible, and bed a replacement tile in place.

Fig 263 With floor tiles, use a brick bolster to chip out the old tile. Take care not to damage its neighbours as you work.

Fig 264 Then bed the replacement into the recess, making sure it sits level with its neighbours so it is not a trip hazard.

Fig 265 Remove old silicone sealant between tiles and sanitary fittings with a sharp chisel. Then pipe a new bead of sealant into place along the joint.

Lifting Old Floorcoverings

One of the biggest problems with laying new floorcoverings is dealing with what was laid previously. Sometimes removing the old floorcovering is quite simple, as in taking up an old carpet; all you have to do is to lift it off its gripper strips or prise out the tacks securing it to the floor, roll it up and carry it outside. Sometimes, what's there can happily stay; many a house has a layer of vinyl floor tiles stuck forever to the concrete ground floor. But there are times when you have to lift an existing floorcovering, either to replace it with something else or to gain access to the space beneath the floor – for example, if you are carrying out alterations or repairs to pipework or cables concealed below the surface.

What to do

As already mentioned, you can in certain circumstances leave some floorcoverings in place, so long as they are well stuck down and present a level surface. Examples include vinyl and cork tiles, sheet vinyl floorcoverings that have been stuck down all over, and ceramic or quarry tiles laid on a solid concrete floor. The latter should, however, be screeded over with a self-smoothing compound to leave a smooth, level surface for the new floorcovering.

If you have to lift cork or vinyl, start at an edge and use heat from a hot air gun to help soften the adhesive so you can prise the tile or sheet up bit by bit. NEVER try to use solvents such as petrol or white spirit to try to dissolve the adhesive. If tiles were laid over a hardboard underlay, it is quicker to rip up tiles and underlay in one go.

To remove ceramic or quarry tiles, smash one or two with a club hammer to give you a starting point, then use a brick bolster and club hammer to prise the tiles up row by row, working across the room. If they were laid over a plywood underlay, it is again quicker to prise this up with a crowbar; the tiles will probably burst off the boards anyway as you lift them.

Lift timber block floors by prising up individual blocks with a claw hammer.

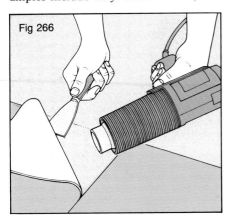

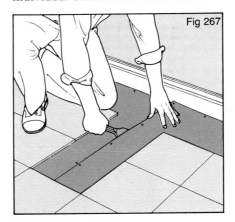

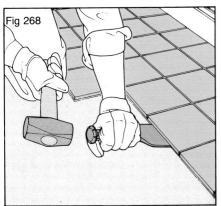

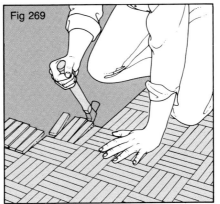

Fig 266   Use heat from a hot air gun to soften the adhesive so you can prise up sheet vinyl or vinyl tiles. NEVER try to use solvents such as petrol, which will not work and could cause an explosion.

Fig 267   If the tiles have been laid on a hardboard underlay, it is far quicker to prise this up after removing a few tiles along the board edges for access.

Fig 268   Use a brick bolster and club hammer to lift old ceramic or quarry floor tiles.

Fig 269   Prise up parquet panels with a claw hammer or crowbar if they are damaged or show signs of lifting.

Repairing Damaged Floorcoverings

Floorcoverings, like wallcoverings, can suffer accidental damage or premature wear, and some first aid is the solution both to restore the surface's looks and, in some cases, to stop them being a trip hazard.

The biggest problem with trying to make repairs lies in finding suitable materials to patch the damage. With sheet and tile materials, it always pays to keep offcuts or spares for this eventuality, but few people are so far-sighted. That leaves two choices; to hunt for suitable replacements in the shops, or to cannibalize what you already have by lifting small areas of repair material from beneath fitted furniture or in an unseen corner.

What to do

To patch damaged **sheet vinyl** flooring, lay a matching offcut over the damaged area, aligning the pattern carefully if there is one, and cut through both layers with a sharp knife and a straightedge. Cut along obvious pattern lines if possible. Then lift the cut-out, brush some floorcovering adhesive onto the floor surface and beneath the edges of the cut-out, and press the patch into place. Weight it down overnight to ensure a good bond to the floor.

You can use a variation on this technique to patch **carpets**, sticking the patch in place with double-sided carpet tape.

With **cork and vinyl tiles**, try to lift the whole tile so you can glue down a replacement. Make cuts across the centre of the tile, then start lifting it from the centre with a broad-bladed scraping knife, using heat from a hot air gun or even a domestic iron to soften the adhesive. Scrape off as much adhesive as possible before bedding the new tile in place.

With **timber panel** floors, use a sharp wood chisel to dig out any damaged fingers and the remains of the adhesive or backing beneath. Then cut a new piece of matching wood (stained first if necessary to get a good colour match) and glue it into place level with its neighbours.

For advice on repairing ceramic tiled floors (see page 82).

What you need:
- straightedge
- sharp handyman's knife
- offcut of sheet vinyl floorcovering
- offcut of wood to match damaged panel
- old chisel
- flooring adhesive
- adhesive spreader

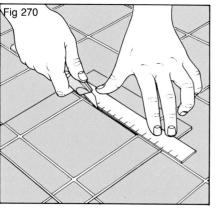

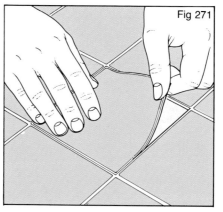

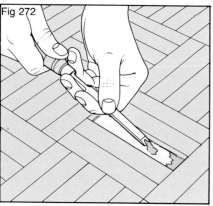

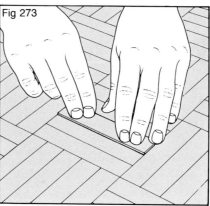

Fig 270 You can patch damaged sheet vinyl if you have a matching offcut. Lay the offcut over the damaged area, align the pattern carefully and cut through both layers with a sharp knife and a straightedge. Then lift the square surrounding the damage.

Fig 271 Scrape away any adhesive below the damaged area, then stick the patch in place with flooring adhesive.

Fig 272 You can repair damaged parquet panels by chiselling out the damaged finger and its adhesive.

Fig 273 Cut a matching finger of wood, stained if necessary to match the rest of the floor, and glue it into place.

EXPENSIVE JOBS

However competent a do-it-yourselfer you are, there will be some jobs that are either too big for you to tackle or require professional skills and equipment. Examples include such major tasks as painting the outside of the house, large-scale interior decorating or laying certain types of floor-coverings – all jobs which may not be beyond your skill if you are a very experienced decorator, but which are likely to take too long if tackled on a DIY basis. In all these cases you may prefer to call in an outside contractor to do the work for you. This is a move that many people regard with some trepidation, since finding good, reliable tradesmen can be difficult and choosing the wrong firm could result not only in a bodged job but in considerable financial loss as well.

Here are some general guidelines to help you minimize the risk of picking a cowboy, followed by a look at what's involved in employing professionals.

Finding a Contractor

Once you have decided you need to call in a professional, your first step is to get people with the skills you require to visit the site and give you a firm quotation for the job.

Personal recommendation is by far the best and safest way of finding someone suitable. If a firm has already carried out work for friends, relatives or neighbours you will be able to get a first-hand account of its performance and even to check up on the standard of workmanship.

If this does not work, your next step is to take a walk or a drive round your area, looking for signs of someone carrying out the sort of work you want done. Many firms now put up a sign outside the site they are working on (or park their vans close by), and will not mind if you approach them. You can do this directly, or you can telephone the number on the sign or van. You can also approach householders directly if it is obvious that they have recently completed work similar to that which you want doing. Most people are only too happy to show off a job well done and to put you in touch with the contractor concerned.

Fig 274 (*above*) One major task many householders prefer to leave to a professional is exterior decorating, usually because of the sheer scale of the job.

Next, try your Yellow Pages or Thomson Local telephone directory. Both list local contractors by trades, and many of the display advertisements not only give more details of the sort of work undertaken, but may also reveal whether the firm is a member of a relevant trade association (see below). With this method, it is well worth asking the firm about other jobs it has done locally. Any company worth its salt will be please to put you in touch with satisfied customers.

Your last method of contact with local contractors is via the various professional and trade associations to which many reputable companies and individuals belong. These associations will give you the names and addresses of their members working in your area, and some offer other back-up services such as guarantees and arbitration schemes which may be worth knowing about. Membership of such a body is generally a good sign (many require evidence of several years' trading and satisfactory accounts before granting membership), but it's wise to check firms who claim membership with the body concerned – some firms simply 'borrow' logos and claim membership to enhance their image. For more details about individual decorating and related trade associations, see page 94.

Getting and Assessing Quotations

Once you have contacted someone who sounds interested in carrying out whatever work you want done, your next job is to explain clearly what the job involves and to find out as precisely as possible what it is going to cost you, when work can start and how long it will take to complete. For major projects such as painting the house or laying fitted carpets it is essential not to rely on verbal agreements, but to ensure that everything is in writing. This can save a lot of argument, and will also help a court to sort a dispute out if things go seriously wrong. First, make sure that you understand the meaning of the following terms, so you know what you are asking for and what the contractor intends you to get.

- *Estimates* are just that − an educated guess as to the rough cost of the job. They are not legally binding.
- *Quotations* are firm offers to carry out a specified job for an agreed price. A quotation for a simple job should include details of material costs.
- *Tenders* are also offers to carry out specified work for a named price, but are understood to involve an element of competition with other contractors.

Most contractors will want to make a site visit to assess the scale of the job involved before even giving an estimate. Explain in as much detail as possible what you require, and tell him you must have a firm quotation for the work, plus details of when he will start and how long the job will take.

Ask at this point whether he or the firm is registered for VAT, and if so whether VAT is payable on the work you are having done. Generally speaking, you do not have to pay VAT on work involving the construction, alteration or demolition of a building, but VAT *is* payable on repair works and maintenance. If he is not a registered VAT trader (with a registration number printed on his notepaper), he cannot charge you VAT on work he does for you.

Always get at least two quotations for the job, and more if you can. This allows you to compare terms as well as prices before making your choice. Impossibly high quotes rarely mean you will get top-quality work; they are the contractor's way of saying he does not want the job, but will do it if you are prepared to pay a silly price.

Once you have received the quotations, study them carefully. The amount of detail given will vary from firm to firm, but they should cover the following points:

- a description of the work to be carried out, preferably presented as a detailed list setting out all the stages involved.
- details of particular materials or fittings to be used for the project, and who will supply them.
- who will be responsible for obtaining any official permission needed.
- when the work will start.
- when the work will be completed.
- who will be responsible for insuring the work and materials on site.
- whether sub-contractors will be employed, and for which parts of the job.
- how variations to methods, timing or costs will be agreed.
- the total cost of the work.
- when payment will be required.

These details form part of the contract between you and whoever you decide to employ, so it is important that they are discussed and dealt with now, to prevent arguments later. Some firms may include them on a standard form of contract sent with the quotation, or may print their terms and conditions on the reverse of their quotation. In either case, read them carefully; now is the time to discuss any clauses you do not want to apply.

Once you have received quotations from the various firms you approached, it is up to you to decide which one to accept on the basis of price, timing and other factors such as your personal impressions or any recommendations you have received. When you have made your choice, write and accept the quotation . . . and notify unsuccessful applicants as a courtesy.

You now have a contract between yourself and the contractor. In most circumstances there is no reason to suppose that anything will go wrong but if it does, tackle it immediately so things can be put right. Mention problems verbally first of all, and if this does not resolve matters, follow up with a letter outlining the nature of your complaint and requesting specific action to correct it. Always keep notes of any discussions you have with the contractor, and copies of any letters you send, in case a dispute cannot be resolved and you have to go to independent arbitration.

FACTS AND FIGURES

This section is intended as a handy reference guide to the range of decorating materials you will need to carry out the various jobs described earlier in the book. It will help you to see at a glance what is available and in what sizes or quantities, so you can plan your requirements in detail and draw up itemised shopping lists for individual decorating projects.

Lastly, on page 94 there is a detailed glossary of all the terms used in the book, as well as a list of useful addresses.

Paint for Walls

Emulsion paint is the most widely used product, intended for decorating walls and ceilings with a plaster or plasterboard surface. It consists of a mixture of pigments and binders in an emulsion with water, and dries by evaporation – far more quickly than solvent-based types, and without their characteristic paint odour. Since the paint is water-based, it can be cleaned from painting equipment with water – more convenient than solvent-based types.

Emulsion paint is sold in matt and silk versions, the latter drying to a finish with a distinct sheen. Many emulsions have non-drip additives, making them easier to apply generously for one-coat cover, and some come as roller paint in semi-solid form too. An enormous colour range is available, usually in sizes of 1, 2½ and 5 litres (1¾, 4½ and 9 pints). Coverage on smooth surfaces is around 15sq m (160sq ft) per litre for ordinary 'runny' types, and about 11sq m (120sq ft) per litre for non-drip types.

Paint for Wood and Metal

Gloss paint is a term used to describe solvent-based paint that dries to a high gloss finish – the traditional paint for wood and metal inside and outside the house. Gloss paints were originally based on linseed oil (hence the term oil paint) but now contain synthetic resins of various types such as alkyd and polyurethane. They dry partly by evaporation, partly by chemical action, to form a film that's more hard-wearing than water-based paint; however, they take longer to dry and have

Fig 275 (*above*) Which paint? Which colour? How much? What primer? What undercoat? There are plenty of questions that need answering before any decorating project gets underway.

to be washed out of painting equipment with a solvent such as white spirit or paraffin unless they have been modified to allow hot soapy water to be used. The surface beneath must be treated with an appropriate primer and an undercoat before the gloss top coat is applied.

As with emulsion, non-drip versions are available as well as traditional 'runny' types. Tin sizes generally start at 500ml (just under 1 pint), although smaller tinlets are also available. Coverage is around 15sq m (160sq ft) per litre for non-drip ones.

Eggshell paint is a solvent-based paint that dries to a finish with a very slight sheen. It can be used on walls as well as woodwork if a more hard-wearing and stain-resistant finish is required, and has the advantage over gloss paint of disguising surface blemishes on less-than-perfect woodwork. It's available in a wide range of colours, in tins containing 500ml, 1, 2½ and 5 litres. Coverage is around 16sq m (170sq ft) per litre.

Paint for Outside Walls

Masonry paint is used, as its name implies, for painting outside brick, stone, rendering and pebbledashing. The paints usually contain fillers such as finely crushed rock

---

PAINT SIZES

The commonest size of container for gloss and eggshell paints is 1 litre (1¾ pints), and for emulsion 2½ litres (about 4½ pints). Masonry paint is usually sold in 5-litre (9 pint) containers.

Smaller sizes are less widely available for all paint types. You can usually expect to find 500ml (⅞ pint) tins of gloss paint, and 1 litre (1¾ pints) tins for emulsion.

Larger sizes are generally restricted to white and a few popular colours.

or chopped fibres, which help bridge fine cracks in the wall surface. For this reason, a special nozzle must be used if they are to be applied with a spray gun, since the fillers would quickly clog a conventional nozzle. They can, of course, be applied by brush or roller too.

Masonry paints are available in a range of mainly subdued colours. Usually the smallest available tin size is 5 litres; coverage depends to a large extent on the roughness and porosity of the surface, and ranges from around 5sq m (55sq ft) per litre on rough surfaces, up to 15sq m (160sq ft) per litre on smooth ones.

Primers and Undercoats

Primers provide a base coat that will stick firmly to the surface being painted, ready for the undercoat and top coat that follow. They also help to seal porous surfaces, and prevent substances such as resin and fugitive colours from bleeding through the paint. There is a wide range of types for different surfaces.

Ordinary softwood and man-made boards should be primed with wood primer or a combined primer/undercoat. Hardwoods and resinous softwoods should be treated with aluminium wood primer.

New plaster should be treated with an all-purpose primer, porous or powdery plaster and rendering with a stabilizing primer.

New iron and steel should be primed with calcium plumbate primer out of doors, zinc chromate primer indoors (for a lead-free finish). Calcium plumbate primer should also be used on galvanized surfaces, zinc phosphate on aluminium. Lead, copper and brass need no priming.

Primers are sold in tins ranging from 500ml upwards. Coverage varies widely, from as little as 6sq m per litre for stabilizing primer on porous surfaces up to around 15sq m per litre for most wood and metal primers.

Undercoat is a paint applied over the appropriate primer on wood, metal or plasterwork, ready for the final top coat. It contains a high proportion of pigment, which helps obliterate the colour beneath; ideally the undercoat colour should be a reasonable match for that of the final top coat. It also fills minor defects in the surface and helps the top coat to adhere well.

Where water-based paints are being used on woodwork, an acrylic primer/undercoat is generally used; with gloss and eggshell finishes a solvent-based undercoat is preferred. On walls being painted with emulsion paint, diluted emulsion is used as the undercoat.

Varnishes and Stains

Varnish is a clear sealer used as a decorative finish on wood where the grain pattern is to remain visible. Most are solvent-based, although acrylic and water-based varieties are becoming more widespread. The commonest type is made using polyurethane resins, which are very hard-wearing and so are ideal for use on surfaces such as floors and furniture. However, they are not easy to recoat satisfactorily when they have weathered out of doors, and traditional oil or alkyd resin varnishes are preferred here.

Varnishes are also available with added pigments, and are known as coloured sealers; they do not give the same depth of colour as stains and clear varnish used separately.

Clear varnishes and coloured sealers are available in matt, satin and gloss finishes. Tin sizes range from 250ml (½ pint) upwards; coverage is generally about 15sq m per litre.

Stains are colouring agents used on wood to alter its natural colour without hiding the grain pattern. Two types are available – water-based and spirit-based – and both come in a range of wood shades and in a number of bold primary colours. Different colours of the same type can be mixed to provide intermediate shades and either type can be thinned with the appropriate solvent to weaken the depth of colour. Once staining is complete, the surface must be sealed to protect it. Wood stains are sold in small containers of up to 250ml (½ pint).

COVERAGE

Coverage obviously depends on several factors, including the roughness and porosity of the surface to which it is being applied and the thickness of the coating. The following figures are intended as a rough guide to the coverage you can expect from a litre of the product; always check the manufacturer's coverage figure printed on the container you are buying.

Liquid gloss	16sq m
Non-drip gloss	13sq m
Eggshell	12sq m
Matt emulsion	15sq m
Silk emulsion	14sq m
Non-drip emulsion	12sq m
Undercoat	11sq m
Wood primer	12sq m
Primer/u'coat	11sq m
Metal primer	10sq m
Stabilizing primer	6sq m
Masonry paint	5–10sq m
Varnish	20sq m

Wallcoverings

Almost all types of wallcoverings are sold in standard rolls 10.05m (33ft) long and about 530mm (20¾in) wide. A few more expensive types, especially fabric wallcoverings, come in wider widths and are usually sold by the metre (3ft 3in).

Patterned Papers

Wallpaper is paper with a printed pattern on the surface, which may be flat or embossed. It's available in a huge range of patterns, and is the least expensive decorated wallcovering around (except when it's hand-printed). However, it's not washable or particularly stain-resistant, so should not be used in areas where moisture or heavy wear are likely.

Washable wallpaper is printed wallpaper with a transparent protective film on the surface, which makes it resistant to stains and relatively easy to wash if it is marked. Some types are ready-pasted.

Vinyl wallcoverings consist of a layer of polyvinyl chloride (vinyl) on which the printed design is fused, and a paper backing that is pasted in the usual way. Some are ready-pasted. They are one of the most hard-wearing wallcoverings – the vinyl surface can be cleaned vigorously to remove stains and marks without fear of damaging the pattern. They are also among the easiest to strip, since the vinyl layer can simply be peeled off dry from the paper backing.

Foil wallcoverings consist of a metallized plastic film on a paper backing, and are often overprinted with patterns. The surface is resistant to moisture, though is generally not as hard-wearing as a vinyl wallcovering, and since the foil conducts electricity the wallcovering should be hung with care behind light switch and power point faceplates.

Novamura is the brand name of a unique all-plastic wallcovering made from foamed polyethylene and printed with a range of surface designs. It is extremely light, and is hung directly onto wall or ceiling surfaces by pasting them, not the wallcovering. It's warm to the touch but rather fragile.

Papers to Paint Over

Relief wallcoverings have a three-dimensional surface, formed either by embossing or by the inclusion of things like woodchips in the paper.

Embossed wallpaper has a three-dimensional surface formed by passing the paper between embossing rollers during manufacture. The embossing may be a random effect or a regular formal pattern. Plain types such as Anaglypta and Supaglypta are intended for overpainting; printed types often have the embossing in register with the printed design. They need careful hanging to avoid flattening the embossing, and are prone to damage from knocks and rubbing in use.

Woodchip wallpaper is a thick pulpy wallpaper containing small woodchips which give it a surface texture resembling coarse oatmeal.

Lining paper is a plain, porous wallpaper used to provide a smooth surface of uniform porosity on walls and ceilings, ready for subsequent paper-hanging. Several different grades are available for light, medium and heavy-duty applications, and there is a special extra-white grade intended to be used when a painted finish is required instead.

Exotica

Fabric wallcoverings are made by bonding plain or patterned fabrics to a paper backing for ease of hanging. Hessian is the commonest type, but a number of more expensive types are also available. Most have to be edge-trimmed after hanging, and should be hung with a thick ready-mixed wallpaper paste.

Flock wallcoverings have a surface pattern consisting of areas of raised pile of wool, silk or synthetic fibres which have been bonded to the paper backing. Ordinary flock wallpapers are expensive and extremely delicate, but modern vinyl flocks have the pile areas fused into the vinyl surface of the wallcovering and are tough enough to withstand washing.

How Many Rolls?

Wall height from skirting	Measurement round room (including doors and windows)										
	10	11	12	13	14	15	16	17	18	19	20m
2.0–2.2m	4	5	5	5	6	6	6	6	7	7	8
2.2–2.4m	4	5	5	6	6	6	7	7	8	8	9
2.4–2.6m	5	5	6	6	7	7	8	8	9	9	10
2.6–2.8m	5	6	6	7	7	8	8	9	9	10	11
2.8–3.0m	5	6	7	7	8	8	9	9	10	11	12

ROLL SIZES
Nearly all wallcoverings are sold in standard-sized rolls measuring 10.05m (33ft) long and 520–530mm (about 21 in) wide. Some materials such as fabric wallcoverings are generally sold by the metre and roll widths vary; check when you buy.

TIP
When you redecorate a room with a wallcovering, make a note on the top edge of the room door of how many rolls you used so you will not have to measure up again next time.

Tiles for Walls, Cladding and Coving

Apart from ceramic tiles, there are several other products that are available for decorating wall and ceiling surfaces around the house.

Tiles for Walls

Ceramic tiles for walls are small squares or rectangles of fired clay with a glazed surface that may be plain or patterned. They are generally about 4mm (just over ⅛in) thick.

Most wall tiles nowadays are of the universal type, which means that they are glazed on at least two adjacent edges, and sometimes on all four edges. This means they can be used at the perimeter of tiled areas, where the tile edges will be visible. Before their introduction, special round-edged tiles were used here.

They are stuck to the wall with special tile adhesive; waterproof types are available for use in areas such as kitchens and bathrooms where the tiled surface is likely to get wet.

The most common size for wall tiles is 150mm (6in) square, but smaller 108mm (4¼in) squares and various rectangular shapes are also widely available.

Mosaics are tiny pieces of ceramic tile made in a range of square, round and interlocking geometric shapes. They are usually mounted on a fabric backing for ease of handling, and are fixed using conventional ceramic tile adhesive. After laying, the gaps between the individual mosaic pieces are filled with grout.

Cork wall tiles come in a range of different natural shades, and the cork may also be stained with primary colours during manufacture. Tile thickness ranges from about 3mm (⅛in) for plain tiles up to around 12mm (1½in) for softer types intended for use as pinboards.

The commonest tile size is 300mm (12in) square, but other sizes of squares and rectangles are available. The tiles are generally stuck in place with a contact adhesive, which makes them difficult to remove if you want to redecorate.

Cladding and Wallboards

Cladding is a wall finish formed by fixing either timber planks or wallboards to a wall surface as an alternative to a traditional plaster finish. Planks can be used on both interior and exterior walls.

The boards are usually profiled – with interlocking tongue-and-groove edges or overlapping ones such as shiplap. They are nailed to a groundwork of timber battens so that each successive board conceals the fixing of the previous one. The boards are stocked in a range of profiles by timber merchants, and are bought by the unit (300mm). Board widths are usually a nominal 100 or 150mm (4 or 6in), but the actual size is reduced by up to 10mm (⅜in) by the profiling.

Wallboards are man-made boards with a decorative facing used to line walls and ceilings in much the same way as cladding. They have either a hardboard or a plywood backing, and the face may be of natural wood veneer or a plastic film imitating materials such as tiles, tongue-and-groove cladding or even brickwork. They are sold in standard 2,440 x 1,220mm (8 x 4ft) sheets, and sometimes in smaller half and quarter-sheet panels.

Ceiling Decoration

Cornice and coving are decorative mouldings used to finish off the angle between walls and ceilings. The terms are often interchanged, although strictly speaking a cornice is a projecting moulding on the exterior of a building.

These mouldings used to be formed in situ by plasterers, but nowadays are sold in lengths ready to be fixed directly into position. There are four main types. The cheapest is made from expanded polystyrene, and generally comes in a plain quadrant type only; prefabricated internal and external mitres are needed to turn the moulding round corners.

Similar but larger quadrant mouldings are formed in the same way as plasterboard, with a paper skin enclosing a plaster core. These are not a solid quadrant; one edge is stuck to the wall surface, the other to the ceiling, leaving a triangular space behind.

Ornate coving mouldings are available in a wide range of traditional patterns. These are made either from fibrous plaster, which is very heavy and rather expensive, or in lightweight urethane foam with a smooth surface skin – cheaper, and easier to fix in place.

All types are bought by the metre, or are available in standard lengths – usually 2m (6ft 6in).

Sheet Floorcoverings

Only two sheet floorcovering materials are widely used in the home – carpets and sheet vinyl. Both come in a huge range of colours, designs and surface textures, and provide a seam-free floorcovering in all but the largest rooms.

Carpets

Carpets are floorcoverings consisting of fibre tufts or loops woven or stuck to a durable backing. Woven carpets are generally the most expensive, and are made by either the Axminster or the Wilton method. Tufted carpets are made by stitching tufts of fibre into a woven backing, where they are secured by adhesive. Some cheaper types have a foam underlay bonded directly to the backing; others require a separate underlay.

A wide range of fibre types is used in carpet construction today, including wool, nylon, acrylic, polypropylene and viscose rayon. Fibre blends can improve carpet performance; a mixture of 80 per cent wool and 20 per cent nylon is particularly popular for providing a combination of warmth, resilience, wear, low flammability and resistance to soiling.

Pile length and density affect the carpet's performance as well as its looks. The pile can be cut (often to different lengths, giving a sculpture effect), looped (uncut and left long), corded (uncut and pulled tight to the backing) or twisted. A dense pile wears better than a loosely-woven one; it should not be possible to see the backing easily when the pile is parted with the fingers.

Carpet widths are described as broadloom (more than 1.8m/6ft wide) or body (usually up to 900mm wide). The former are intended for large areas, the latter for corridors and stairs. Most broadloom carpet is in fact made in imperial 12ft (3.66m) and metric 4m (13ft) widths; it is sold by the linear yard or metre.

Sheet Vinyl

Sheet vinyl flooring is the modern equivalent of linoleum, and provides a smooth, hygienic and easy-to-clean floorcovering that is widely used in rooms such as kitchens, bathrooms and hallways. It is made from layers of plastic resins, with a clear wear layer protecting the printed design and frequently with an air cushion

layer between this and the backing for extra comfort and warmth underfoot. It is fairly flexible and easy to cut for an exact fit; it's generally loose-laid, with adhesive or double-sided tape being used only at seams and edges.

Vinyl flooring is available in a wide range of designs, including excellent imitations of ceramic tiles, wood, cork and stone floors. It is sold by the linear metre from rolls 2 or 4m (6ft 6in or 13ft) wide; the larger width enables seam-free floors to be laid in most medium-sized rooms.

Fig 276 (*above*) Always get professional advice when choosing a new carpet, to ensure that the colour or design you have chosen is up to the job.

Fig 277 (*left*) Sheet vinyl flooring is in general very hardwearing, although cushioned types may eventually begin to show indentations in very heavy traffic areas.

Glossary

Alkyd resin Ingredient used as a binder in modern solvent-based paints, in place of linseed oil.

Aluminium wood primer Primer used on resinous hardwoods and to seal bituminous paints and stains.

Anaglypta Trade name for a relief wallcovering made from wood pulp. It is white, and is overpainted once hung.

Artex A trade name for a textured coating used on walls and ceilings. Original Artex is a powder which is mixed with water; most modern textured coatings are sold ready-mixed,

Border Narrow strip of printed wallpaper, used to highlight features such as window openings.

Cladding Timber and wallboards used as a surface decoration for walls. It is usually fixed to a network of battens.

Cornice and coving Terms used interchangeably to describe decorative mouldings of plaster, plasterboard or plastic used to conceal the joint between walls and ceilings.

Cross-lining Hanging lining paper horizontally on wall surfaces prior to hanging another wallcovering over it.

Cushioned vinyl Vinyl floorcovering with a layer of trapped air bubbles incorporated in its construction to improve comfort and insulation underfoot.

Distemper An old-fashioned wall paint rarely used today, but often found beneath old wallpaper. It must be removed or sealed before being decorated over.

Drop pattern wallcovering Wallcovering with a pattern which drops by half a repeat across the width.

Efflorescence White powdery deposit found on wall surfaces that are damp or which have not dried out after replastering work. It should be brushed off dry.

Eggshell paint Solvent-based paint which dries to a sheen rather than a high gloss.

Emulsion paint Water-based paint mainly used on wall and ceiling surfaces. It is thinned and washed from tools with water.

Filler Powder or ready-mixed product used to repair minor damage in plaster and plasterboard surfaces. Fillers are applied with a filling knife, which is more flexible than a stripping knife.

Frieze Narrow strip of printed wallpaper, somewhat wider than a border, used to form decorative bands on walls.

Grout Powder or ready-mixed product used to fill the narrow gaps left after ceramic tiles have been fixed to floors or walls.

Knotting Sealer used to cover knots in woodwork, preventing resin from oozing through and marring the finish.

Lincrusta Relief wallcovering made from a mixture of linseed oil and fillers, hardened like putty and formed into rolls which are hung with special adhesive.

Lining paper Plain wallpaper hung to provide a stable base for other wallcoverings. Special grades are available for overpainting.

Masonry paint Paint for exterior walls, usually water-based and reinforced with fillers and fibres for bridging cracks.

Mastic Flexible sealant used to fill gaps between adjacent surfaces of different materials, such as plaster and wood.

Matt finish paint Solvent or water-based paint that dries to a non-reflective finish.

Novamura Foamed polyethylene wallcovering, hung straight from the roll. It can be dry-stripped.

Primer Liquid used on many bare surfaces to seal them and provide a good base for undercoats and top coats.

Ready-pasted wallcovering Wallcovering coated with dried paste, which is activated by immersing the length to be hung in a trough of water.

Relief wallcovering Embossed material designed to be overpainted once hung. Types include Anaglypta, Supaglypta, Vynaglypta and Lincrusta.

Satin or silk finish paint Solvent or water-based paint that dries to a slight sheen rather than a full gloss finish.

Solvent-based paint Paint mainly used on wood and metal, needing white spirit as a thinner and cleaning agent. Gloss and eggshell paints are of this type.

Textured finish Powder or ready-mixed compound applied to wall and ceiling surfaces and given a random or regular texture.

Vinyl wallcovering Wallcovering with the design printed on a PVC layer which is stuck to a paper backing. The top layer can be stripped dry.

Washable wallpaper Printed paper with a clear plastic surface coating which can be washed and which must be broken up before the paper can be stripped.

Woodchip wallpaper Wallpaper containing coarse wood chips, designed to be overpainted once hung.

Index

Index